OVERCOMING THE 7 DEADLIEST COMMUNICATION SINS

A New Standard for Workplace Communication: Build a Championship Work Environment to Get Things Done and Make More Money

SKIP WEISMAN

Lynx Cat Press
Poughkeepsie, NY

This book is dedicated to M&M,
better known to others as Martha and Mel.
Or, more commonly referred to by me,
my older brother Harry,
and older sisters Jane and Marlene,
as Mom and Dad.

CONTENTS

PART I.

THE CASE FOR A NEW
STANDARD FOR WORKPLACE
COMMUNICATION

"It is a matter of conversation that ultimately gets people to converge on common projects and common values. So all we have is conversation. And when conversation fails all we have is violence. There [are] just two modes, conversation and violence."

— Sam Harris, The Waking Up Podcast[1]

---

1. Harris, Sam. "Episode 90: Living With Violence." Interview. *Waking Up Podcast* (audio blog), August 6, 2017. https://samharris.org/podcasts/living-with-violence/. I heard this comment from Sam Harris on his Waking Up podcast. He said this in relation to violence in the world caused by religious fundamentalism, and also regarding the polarization of society today. I immediately thought it relevant to some of today's workplaces, if we just substitute the word "conflict" for "violence."

CHAPTER 1.

THE WAKE UP CALL

"It is paradoxical, yet true, to say, that the more we know, the more ignorant we become in the absolute sense, for it is only through enlightenment that we become conscious of our limitations. Precisely one of the most gratifying results of intellectual evolution is the continuous opening up of new and greater prospects."

— Nikola Tesla

"I want out."

On September 17, 1997, I was taking night classes at a local university to finish my long-overdue master's degree. That night, I got home from class at about 9:15 p.m.

I walked into the house, put my books down on the dining room table, and was confronted by my wife. "Skip, we have to talk, because I want out."

"What do you mean, you want out?" I said.

"I can't take it anymore," she said firmly. "I want a divorce."

Acting the part of the typically-confused, caught-off-guard husband, not grasping what was going on, I was blank-faced as she handed me a book and said, "Read this, then maybe you'll understand."

I looked down at the book; the front cover read, *The Verbally Abusive Relationship*, by Patricia Evans.

I couldn't put it down. I read it in record time.

Every page seemed to recount the details of our marriage. I couldn't deny the behaviors I was reading described how I treated my wife. It seemed as if the book was written about me.

I was embarrassed and appalled. It may have been the most humbling experience of my life.

You will learn a little about how I was verbally abusive later in the book, in *Chapter 8: Lack of Appropriate Tone & Body Language*.

THE BIG BANG

If there was a genesis of my move from the career of my dreams in professional baseball, into my second career as a professional speaker and small business coach, that day, September 17, 1997, was The Big Bang.

The subsequent experience of my divorce–and the personal development and self-awareness–propelled me on this new career and business path.

It started with couples' counseling, trying to save the relationship, which also included individual counseling. We tried for about two months. For a number of reasons, though, it didn't work. In the end, it led to what was for the best for both of us.

We separated after the two months, but I continued my individual counseling. At some point, Chuck (my counselor) and I spoke about the book my wife had given me; I remember the conversation clearly.

"You know, I grew up in a verbally abusive household. My mother was always yelling. It was embarrassing during the summer with the windows open in the house," I explained. "Our whole neighborhood could hear her."

Chuck responded, "Yeah, I could see how that would impact you as a young child.

"But," he went on, "you are not a young child anymore, and you can choose to communicate differently, if you'd like."

"What do you mean?" I asked, trying to understand.

"Well," he continued, "you're not living with your mother anymore, and you've been on your own for 20 years. You're an adult, and can make different choices now."

"I *can?*"

"Certainly," he said patiently. "You really should stop blaming your mother for choices *you* are making now as an adult."

I thought for a moment. "But, when I get upset, my emotions take over, and I react the way my mother always did."

"I can help you with that," he said, "but first, *you* have to decide you don't want to be like your mother anymore."

"That's easy," I said. "I hate being like this."

Thus began my journey to becoming a workplace communication expert. Chuck taught me I could have control over my communication style. He showed me how it was my self-communication that led to my lack of control over my emotions.

Chuck said, "All of your success (and you've been pretty successful in your career), and all of your failures and frustrations, are all directly related to communication in some way. It's the same for everyone.

"It's important for you to understand," he said, "you are *always* communicating: you cannot *not* communicate. Even when you're trying *not* to communicate, you are communicating that you don't want to."

Those not-so-little lessons from my relationship counselor opened my mind to the importance of interpersonal communication and how it impacts every facet of our lives.

At about this same time, I got a flyer in the mail announcing peak performance motivational coach Anthony Robbins was coming to my area for a weekend workshop. I signed up.

Within the first few hours of that program, sitting with 2,500 other human beings trying to find answers to all of life's problems, I heard Tony proclaim, "The quality of your life is equal to the quality of your communication."

I thought, *Boy, ain't that the truth.* Tony was reinforcing everything Chuck had told me.

I can't overstate how powerful hearing the same message from two different men around the same time was for me.

That Robbins' seminar was February of 1998. My wife left in early December, launching our official separation. I had found myself on a new path of personal and professional self-discovery, as well as at a career crossroads.

That summer was my 17th season in professional baseball management, and I was beginning to sense I was drifting away from my childhood dream of working in professional sports.

I cared less and less whether my favorite major league sports team–or even my own minor league franchise team–won or lost.

I had bigger problems.

Then, the next Big Bang of my life hit.

A NEW IDENTITY

During a typical summer night at our ballpark in mid-July, our home team was, again, playing in front of a sold-out stadium.

It was the middle of the sixth inning. I was standing at the top of the steps that led down to our left field picnic patio. It was a great perch, where I had the entire stadium in full view. I could enjoy a little bit of the game while having the stadium crowd in front of me, in case I had to react to a situation in the stands. Fans and staff would engage in conversation while I was hanging out.

During a solitary moment, I glanced at the scoreboard.

Our home team was losing 4-2.

Since I didn't wear a watch, I pulled my cell phone out of its holster on my hip to check the time. It was 9:07 p.m.

My next thought changed my life forever.

I don't care if we win or lose. I just want to go home.

That was the beginning of the end of my career in professional baseball.

It turns out, I was confused, lost, and scared.

At 38 years old, my personal identity was slipping away.

I was having a midlife crisis. I decided in that moment it was time to move on.

I was not ready to move on, though.

Not emotionally. Baseball and sports were all I had cared about since I was seven years old. For 30 years, they had been my passion and focus. It was my identity. That's how other people identified with me, too. How could I leave that behind and be happy? Who could I be, if not that person?

Not professionally. For 17 years, I had worked in one industry, doing basically one job. It was all I knew how to do. What else *could* I do? Where else *could* I add value to the world?

Not financially. In sports, all the money goes to the athletes at the major league level. Minor league baseball, where I was, is your typical small business. There was no pension like my dad had as a supermarket butcher, with a union membership and "safety net" for retirement. I had a little money put away and a small investment in the team I was working with, but half of that would now be going to my wife in the divorce.

Where would I go? What would I do? Who would I become? Who *could* I become? What was the next phase of my life?

These were all questions I was seeking answers for, with little success.

I decided 20 years was a nice round number to finish with. Twenty years is typically the first level of retirement for military personnel, for teachers, police, fire professionals, and so on. For me, it would be my point of career demarcation.

I had two-and-a-half years to figure out who I would be.

From that moment on, I went back to school. I immersed myself in learning and understanding the foundations of human motivation and communication.

After three years of studying the strategies of Anthony Robbins, getting my certifications in hypnotherapy and neuro-linguistic programming (NLP), and practicing with some pro bono clients, I was ready.

It was March, 2001. I told the team's principal owner, my boss, that the coming summer was my final season and I would be moving on.

I had a great final season. After the last home game, on August 31, 2001, they threw me a big party with parting gifts.

Eleven days later, on September 11, 2001, our world changed forever.

Three weeks after, I opened my business full-time.

There was no going back.

It's been 17 years now, and what you are going to read in this book is what I've discovered on my own journey of personal communication transformation. This is what I've learned through seeing my clients struggle with the same interpersonal and intrapersonal communication challenges I experienced for the first 40 years of my life.

HOW TO READ AND USE THIS BOOK

What you will be learning about are The 7 Deadliest Communication Sins, and how to overcome them, which include:

- Lack of Specificity
- Lack of Immediacy, Urgency, & Promptness
- Lack of Directness & Candor
- Lack of Respectful Rebuttals
- Lack of Desirable Behaviors
- Lack of Appropriate Tone & Body Language
- Lack of Focused Attention

As you read, you will notice several things:

1. You are both the victim of these seven deadliest communication sins, and the perpetrator.
2. They impact your relationships and results in both your personal and your professional life.
3. These sins are so common and such a part of our vernacular we will never fully eliminate them. The best we can do is become aware of them, and work hard at reducing their frequency and impact.

If you can reduce the frequency and the impact of these seven most-common, most-damaging communication mistakes, it will impact the quality of your life in every context. I firmly believe what I heard Anthony Robbins say to me in that workshop back in 1998: "The quality of your life is equal to the quality of your communication."

A few years ago, more than two decades after earning my bachelor's degree in communication from Ohio University, I began revisiting the topic of communication as a career. I came across a quote from world-renowned social scientist Robert Carkhuff. He wrote, "Every human interaction is for better or worse."

This quote got me thinking. "Every human interaction" is 100% made up of communication, and not all communication is created equal.

This book will provide insights, ideas, tips, tools, and specific communication techniques in seven different categories. My hope is it will give you the edge you need to put the odds back in your favor, building relationships that can accelerate results in your life, business, and career.

THE 3 OUTCOMES OF COMMUNICATION

Responses from participants in my keynotes, seminars, and strategic work sessions have shown me there are three outcomes from interpersonal human communication (See Figure 1).

1. It builds the relationship by fostering trust between you and them.
2. It slowly erodes the relationship by chipping away at the level of trust between you and them.
3. It instantly destroys the relationship and kills trust between you and them.

You've probably noticed two of those communication outcomes are undesirable. This means, in every communication, you are taking a 67% risk of damaging the relationship. This is not the direction you want to be going if you value quality relationships.

ONLY 3 Outcomes From Your Communications

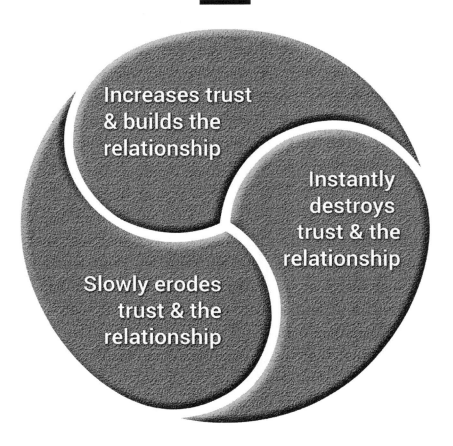

There is a 67% risk of damaging the relationship every time you communicate

Figure 1

This book is divided into four parts.

Part I is about committing to setting a new standard for what you expect from communication from yourself and those around you.

Part II is dedicated to The 3 Primary Communication Sins, which influence overall organizational trust, in addition to trust between individuals in the organization, especially as it pertains to performance management and fairness in the workplace.

Part III will explore The 4 Secondary Communication Sins, which have their biggest and deepest impact on trust between individuals–the severity and the consistency of which determine their impact on the overall environment.

Part IV closes out the book by discussing what is possible when you commit to raising your standard and creating a company culture of "championship communication."

In each of the chapters on The 7 Deadliest Communication Sins, you will learn the manifold ways these communication mistakes manifest in a work environment. Each chapter is backed up by anecdotal case studies as examples, and includes specific strategies, tips, tools, and techniques to communicate in a more effective manner to help you overcome each communication sin.

Each chapter also offers specific solutions to practice, with specific action steps to begin building new habits of communication.

You will also find a set of assessment questions at the end of each chapter to help you identify how you and your organization may be struggling with interpersonal communication and ways you can turn them around. There are also additional resources listed that can further help you in your personal development journey.

But before we get to that, there is one thing you have to do first. As crazy as it sounds, it's to simply change your phone's outgoing voicemail.

CHAPTER 2.

SETTING A NEW STANDARD FOR COMMUNICATION

"More than be rich, more than be famous, more than happy ... I wanted to be great!"

— Bruce Springsteen[1]

If you call my office phone, (845) 463-3838, or my mobile phone (914) 456-6387 (and I encourage you to do so), you will hear the following message:

"I promise to reply to your message by phone, email, or text, within three hours."

People look at me as if I have three heads when I share this in my keynote speeches and seminars. Most audience members tell me, "I could never commit to something like that!"

I empathize with them and say, "It's not about the timeframe; it's about projecting confidence and trust to the other person about you. The key is providing certainty about a timeframe for responding."

---

1. *The Promise: The Making of Darkness on the Edge of Town.* Directed by Thom Zimny. Performed by Bruce Springsteen. USA: Thrill Hill Productions, 2010. DVD.

I always ask, "When you leave a message, wouldn't you at least like some acknowledgement that the person received your message, and either was or wasn't working towards your request?"

That garners almost unanimous agreement.

"So then, you have to give what you want."

I try to break things down for the audience and make it easy for them. I offer three different options.

I say, "You don't have to take my three hours. I realize that may seem extreme to you. So, pick one of these three you think you can commit to."

- 24 hours
- The end of the week
- Three weeks

That last option comes after a long pause, and it always gets a laugh. I'm not serious; I only suggest it to reinforce the point it's not about the time frame.

It is about giving everyone certainty they will hear back from you in a reasonable time. I firmly believe there is no reason why you can't reply within 24 hours. That is the minimum I would expect someone to raise their standard to.

In a business environment where competition is stiff and market differentiation is vital, being responsive to incoming calls is a simple way to raise your standard. By setting a higher standard of expectations for yourself, people will take notice.

When you fulfill that commitment, you will begin to build credibility and trust with those people.

Offering a more specific time frame in your voicemail for callers to expect a reply is a small place to start. I offer it as a simple example for raising the standards of what you expect from communication in your company's work environment.

In what other contexts should you raise the standards for what you expect from communication throughout your company?

MY INSPIRATION

During my final years as a professional baseball CEO, I met Jim Williamson, the new president/CEO of our regional United Way agency.

He is the only person I have ever known to suggest setting this higher standard through changing your voicemail.

I met Jim at a community event. We connected and discussed our common interests as well as ways we could support each other's efforts.

Our team and our local United Way partnered on a number of promotions together, including kicking off their fall fundraising campaign with a major sold-out event at one of our home games.

In my dealings with Jim, he always projected professionalism and high standards. One of the ways he gave that impression was through his outgoing voicemail.

His message promised a return phone call within *four business hours.*

I had never heard anything like that before. *Wow!* I thought. *That is quite a commitment!*

As far as I can remember, he always fulfilled that commitment.

Jim left our community in 2004 to serve in Connecticut as president and CEO of The Community Foundation of Greater New Britain. He retired in 2017, and through the magic of LinkedIn, I was able to reconnect with him.

Even in retirement, he was totally professional, giving credit where credit was due. He told me, "I got that idea from one of our United Way staff members. I immediately saw the value in it, but I didn't know how I could fulfill a commitment like that.

"When I confessed that to my staff member," he continued, "she said, 'You just decide you're going to do it.'

"The concept was perfect for the type of organization I wanted to lead. My goal was to create an organization that other non-profits could emulate by delivering on what we said we would. To do that, we had to set a standard for what we expected from ourselves, first and foremost. This was one way we could set that expectation and project it to the community."

The approach helped Jim create a highly respected, non-profit community organization that historically expected the biggest leaders in their communities to participate in annual fundraising campaigns.

Jim added, "These small things help you build the kind of organization you can trust."

Four years after he began at the organization, another community-wide non-profit commissioned a donor satisfaction survey, and Jim's organization was rated #1 in "professionalism" and "responsiveness."

Small changes like this will help you differentiate yourself and your company. It's a simple shift that can make the biggest difference.

One of my business mentors, Alan Weiss, promises to return calls from his clients within *90* minutes. In all the times we've worked together, he's never failed that commitment.

THE CASE FOR SETTING A HIGHER STANDARD

My favorite movie is Billy Crystal's *City Slickers* (don't judge me–my wife does enough of that regarding my taste in the arts). It's underrated as a movie. Even Gary Keller, the co-founder of Keller Williams Realty, thinks so: he based his entire book, *The One Thing*, on one key message from it.

If you're not familiar with the 1992 movie, Billy Crystal plays a family man, Mitch Robbins, in the midst of a mid-life crisis on his 39th birthday. His long-term friends Phil (played by Daniel Stern) and Ed (Bruno Kirby) give him a gift of a two-week vacation playing cowboy on a cattle drive in the western plains of the United States.

During cowboy training at the ranch the first days of the trip, Mitch is struggling to learn how to rope a cow. In one scene, Ed chastises Mitch for not "getting it."

Mitch shouts back, "Ed, it's not a competition!"

Ed says, "Yes, it is. Everything's a competition! Life's a competition!"

Ed is absolutely right. Life *is* a competition.

Have you ever wanted to pursue a romantic relationship with someone? Did you ever "lose out" to another suitor, though?

I did. It hurt. It was a loss. I lost the competition for the attention of a person I wanted a relationship with.

There is competition in every area of life, including business. If you own a company, you are in competition with other similar companies. When I was in professional baseball, we had no other minor league baseball teams to compete with, but we competed for the family entertainment dollar with other industries that catered to kids and families.

If you're selling a product or service, you are in competition with others who sell similar products or services. If you're a project manager, you are competing with other project managers to lead the next project.

Who is your competition? How do you stack up? What is the gap between you and them? Are you ahead, behind, or equal?

Regardless, if you want to lead the competition, you will need to raise your standard for what you expect of:

1. Yourself
2. Your employees
3. Your work environment

The place to start raising your standard is your communication. It will give you the biggest bang for your investment in time, energy, and resources because it impacts every aspect of your business and life.

I started by borrowing the outgoing voicemail strategy from Jim and Alan. I had two reasons for putting my three-hour reply policy in place:

1. To differentiate myself from the competition:

When prospective clients or other community leaders would call, it would make an immediate and unique memorable impression.

2. To force myself to hold to a higher standard:

When I get the voicemail message, I know the clock is ticking. It forces me to check my voicemail when I'm out of the office if I don't have them forwarded to my cell phone. I typically check voicemail every 90 minutes to two hours when I'm out.

You should do the same for at least those two reasons.

And, you can.

The sad thing is, I've been speaking about this since 2012, and even my closest local business colleagues, who have heard me espouse this strategy, have not yet taken my advice.

That is why I say it is not hard to set yourself apart in today's society. Too many people are too complacent, settling for a low standard that will keep the bar low for themselves.

That is why today is the day you must commit to setting a higher standard for your communication.

Your outgoing voicemail is a simple place to start. You can build from there.

Our society has fallen into a rut of low standards and expectations for interpersonal communication, both in the workplace and at home.

What you will read in the coming chapters will teach you how to set new standards for your communication and those around you.

Additionally, they will help you to overcome the communication challenges and mistakes I see too many business professionals, at all levels, make–The 7 Deadliest Communication Sins.

You may not have realized this, but communication is the cause of every success, failure, and frustration you experience. Therefore, it's time to raise your standard for what you expect from communication from yourself and those around you.

3 CONTEXTS OF COMMUNICATION FOR RAISING STANDARDS

Chances are, you picked up this book because it offered you a promise of improved personal and business performance, which will lead to greater financial rewards.

It can definitely do that for you. But first, it's important to understand where your opportunities for improvement are.

There are three areas to look for ways to raise the standard of communication in your workplace:

1. IT Communication:

Is your technological hardware and software up-to-date? Is it flowing effectively to the people and devices that are connected to it? If not, it is going to cause frustration, and will undermine organizational trust and morale because people don't have the resources to do their job effectively and efficiently.

2. Flow and Process of Communication:

This is a big area of concern that too many organizations fail to invest the time, energy, and focus to discuss. They ignore the issues around who needs to know what and when, and they tolerate the status quo. The excuse is often, "We don't have time to get everyone together."

This is where setting a higher standard can improve your work environment. Set a new standard for what you expect from the process and flow of communication, gain clarity around it, and you will be able to eliminate the time people lost because they were previously chasing information.

Once you commit to that new standard, and you invest time to discuss and make decisions about the flow of communication, you will actually get that time back and more. You have to trust your investment on the front end will pay off when you facilitate the decision-making process, even though it may take multiple iterations to get right.

3. Interpersonal Communication:

Is it positive, productive, and civil? Does it build trust and foster teamwork? If not, it is time to raise the standard. In this book, I will make the case at least 50% or more of your communication issues in your work environment fit into this category.

Raising your standard for expectations around interpersonal communication for yourself and others in your work environment will lead to a high-performance culture that is positive, productive, and more profitable.

For that last reason, this book is going to focus primarily on interpersonal communication.

This book will also focus primarily on interpersonal communication, because when I ask my audiences in keynote addresses and seminars which of those three contexts cause them the biggest problems and the most frustrations, they always respond with "interpersonal communication."

By the end of the book, you will realize there are a significant number of ways you can, and should, be raising your standard of expectations from yourself and those in your work environment in all three contexts of communication. Doing so will give you and your people the technology, the processes, and the resources to allow them to feel good about their work environment, and grow in them a desire to give you their best every day.

WHY COMMUNICATE?

Have you ever asked yourself this question?

Not about specific people, necessarily, but, as a species, why do we communicate?

What is the purpose of human communication?

Why do we communicate?

The main answer is, because it is impossible not to. As my counselor told me, you cannot not communicate. Even when you try not to communicate, you are communicating that you don't want to communicate.

When I ask that question of my audiences during my speeches, I get a lot of different answers, such as:

- To convey information
- To get things I need
- To learn
- To get people to listen to me
- To get people to do things
- For entertainment

All of those are pieces of the reason.

I recently googled "the purpose of communication." There were 1.7 billion possible results. That was too much for me to curate, so I created my own definition:

The purpose of communication is to influence and direct the situations, experiences, and results in your life.

It's that simple. Anything else is superfluous.

If you'd like to better be able to influence and direct the situations, experiences, and results in your life, you must raise your standard for communication and become a much more conscious communicator.

In the following chapters, you will learn about The 7 Deadliest Communication Sins, and the strategies, tips, tools, and techniques for how to overcome them. No matter what your context, understanding them will differentiate you from the competition, as you practice and apply them to build new communication habits.

THE COST OF THE 7 COMMUNICATION SINS

When people experience your new communication habits, your level of credibility will rise–leading to high-trust relationships. And, the first high-trust relationship you will develop is with yourself.

This is more important than you might realize.

Much of the cause of The 7 Communication Sins–which undermine your ability to build the high-trust relationships necessary to fulfill the purpose of communication–is your own self-trust. This is what most people refer to as "self-worth" or "self-esteem."

It is this self-trust, and the trust others will build with you, that allows you to fulfill the purpose of communication. Without credibility and trust, you have no chance to exert the positive influence required to direct the situations, experiences, and results you desire (See Figure 2).

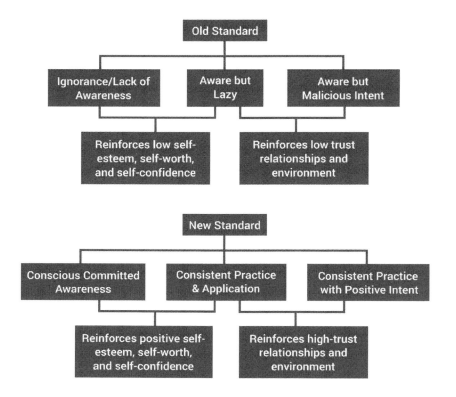

Figure 2

In his book, *The Speed of Trust* (2006), Stephen M.R. Covey offers case studies showing the cost and benefits of trust in an environment. He makes the strong case that, "As trust goes down speed goes down, and costs go up." And, conversely, "as trust goes up speed goes up and costs go down."

Covey is suggesting a very strong correlation between trust and financial impact. Which, in turn, suggests an even stronger correlation between communication (which is the foundation of trust), and financial impact.

To make the case for making a commitment to raising your standard of communication, let's evaluate the cost of poor, ineffective, and/or negative, malicious communication in your work environment (caused by low-trust, low-morale relationships and environments).

What do you think low trust and other aspects of poor, ineffective, and/or maliciously negative communication may be costing *your* company?

One way to get a rough estimate of the cost is to assess these figures (See Figure 3.1 as an example):

1. Estimate the number of hours per week the average employee wastes due to poor, ineffective, and/or maliciously negative communication.
2. Identify the average hourly salary and benefits package for those employees at your company.
3. Multiply the product of those two figures by the number of weeks per year the average employee works.
4. Multiply that figure by the total number of employees in your department, team, or organization overall (whatever entity you are evaluating).

You may want to make copies of the Communication Cost Calculator (See Figure 3.2).

Communication Cost Calculator

The Cost of Poor, Ineffective and/or Maliciously Negative Communication in Your Workplace

1 Average number of hours per week the average employee wastes due to poor, ineffective, and/or maliciously negative communication in your workplace.
___10___ hours

2 $ __25__ / hour

3 Answer to #1 ___10___ x Answer to #2 $___25___ =
$_____250_____ /week

4 Answer from #3 $_____250_____ x #Weeks Worked per year ____50____ = $___12500___/year

5 Answer from #4 $___12500___ x # of total employees ____25____ = $___312,500___ total cost of lost productivity to organization.

Figure 3.1 (example)

Communication Cost Calculator

The Cost of Poor, Ineffective and/or Maliciously Negative Communication in Your Workplace

1 Average number of hours per week the average employee wastes due to poor, ineffective, and/or maliciously negative communication in your workplace.
_____ hours

2 $ _____ / hour

3 Answer to #1 _____ x Answer to #2 $_____ =
$_____ /week

4 Answer from #3 $_____ x #Weeks Worked per year _____ = $_____/year

5 Answer from #4 $_____ x # of total employees _____ = $_____ total cost of lost productivity to organization.

Figure 3.2

Once you realize the cost of poor, ineffective, maliciously negative communication (caused by low-trust, low-morale relationships and environments) you'll be ready to evaluate the quality of communication so you know where to start improving.

Answer the following questions to help you plug your challenges into their respective communication sins. This will enable you to begin applying the solutions you will learn in each of the chapters.

1. What are the frustrations, challenges, issues, and upsets you have with interpersonal communication as you engage and interact with others in your sphere of influence?
2. What are the things regarding interpersonal communication with others you are tolerating that you wish you could change, fix, and/or make better?
3. What are the costs of those interpersonal communication challenges to your business or career? (See your answers from Figure 3.2)

It's the answers to those questions that have brought you to this book.

Realize, if you feel you are tolerating certain communication issues with others, others are most likely feeling the same about you.

The only way that dynamic is going to improve is if one of you changes the way you are communicating, and raises their standard for what they expect from their own communication as well as from others.

Since you're the one reading this book, it's on you.

I've written this book because I don't want you to be like me.

As you read in Chapter 1, my own communication habits were causing the issues in my environment, and even though I thought I had the situations under control, ultimately I lost not only my marriage, but any illusion that I had any control.

My hope is my story in Chapter 1 and this chapter can be your wake up call to commit to that new standard.

From here, the rest of the book will guide you toward ways to set that new standard for yourself and those around you. You will soon understand the seven most common and most damaging communication mistakes we all make, and strategies, tips, tools, and techniques you can immediately apply to counteract them.

Unfortunately, we will never be able to eliminate these sins entirely.

However, as we grow our awareness and build new and better communication habits, we will be able to reduce the frequency and impact of those mistakes, and improve relationships in every area of our lives.

That is why raising your standard for what you expect from communication is vital. When you commit to raising your standard of what you expect from communication in your work environment, it will improve positivity, productivity, and profits at your company.

When you raise your communication standards and complete your transformation by integrating the solutions to The 7 Deadliest Communication Sins, you and those in your work environment will build new habits of communicating. These will develop three vital values that will transform results for your company (See Figure 4):

A NEW STANDARD FOR YOUR ORGANIZATION

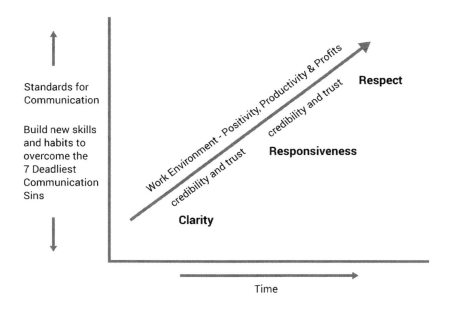

Standards for Communication

Build new skills and habits to overcome the 7 Deadliest Communication Sins

Work Environment - Positivity, Productivity, Productivity & Profits

credibility and trust

Respect

Responsiveness

Clarity

Time

Figure 4

1. Clarity

As you will learn in Chapter 3: Lack of Specificity, clarity is key. My colleague, Ann Latham, points out in her book, *The Clarity Papers*, "there is simply no substitute for knowing what you are trying to accomplish… clarity generates better, faster results."

Without specificity, there can be no clarity. Other sins impacting clarity you will learn include Lack of Directness and Candor, Lack of Desirable Behaviors, and Lack of Focused Attention.

2. Responsiveness

One of the biggest frustrations of small business leaders and their employees I hear is a lack of responsiveness. There is too much waiting and chasing in work environments today.

When you begin building new habits around the skills that overcome The 7 Deadliest Communication Sins, that will change. The specificity that leads to the clarity you need, along with the high-trust relationships and environment it will create, will exponentially raise the responsiveness in the people around you. This will work with your employees, your bosses, your customers, your vendors (and your spouses, significant others, and children too).

Imagine what life and business will be like when you can stop waiting and chasing as people begin responding. How much more business will you generate when your responsiveness blows away that of your competitors because you've raised your standard for what you expect from yourself, your team members, and your clients?

One of my clients, Jay, who you will read about in Chapter 4, is the president of a small manufacturing firm. In our work together, he decided to focus on a huge aspiration: to turn around every quote within 24 hours. We're not there yet, but we're light years ahead of where we were 12 months ago when we first started working together. We've raised the expectation for communication in Jay's work environment, and enhanced responsiveness has been a byproduct of that work. It can be for your organization, too.

3. Respect

This is the secret sauce of all of communication. Many people believe it's trust–and I agree, trust is also very important. I'm confident we could have a spirited debate on what comes first. You may see it as a chicken and egg conundrum. But, I believe respect is the holy grail here.

The reason is, in every work environment I've ever facilitated a strategic planning session (which is in the dozens), respect is always on the list of values people want and expect in their work environment. Whenever I facilitate a program to improve communication in a work environment, and whenever I have conversations with people in toxic work environments, all any of them really want and ask for is that communication be respectful.

There doesn't seem to be enough respectful communication in a work environment today.

It can always be better.

To get there, we need to build a more trusting environment; from credibility and trust, respect will come. Trust is the currency that buys respect.

When you build your work environment around the strategies that overcome The 7 Deadliest Communication Sins, what I term The 7 Critical Communication Skills, you will create a high-trust work environment where everyone operates believing in the credibility of their co-workers, which fosters the respect everyone wants and deserves (See Figure 5).

When you raise your standard of communication, these three values–clarity, responsiveness, and respect–will also help you build your credibility and lead to higher levels of trust with your colleagues, coworkers, direct reports, bosses, and even family members.

Communication may be a "soft" skill, but it pays very "hard" quantifiable dividends when done right.

A NEW STANDARD FOR YOURSELF

Figure 5

Warm Up Exercise

1 In what specific ways are interpersonal communication with others challenging for you? What do others do when communicating with you directly, or what in and around your environment, bothers you? What you are tolerating? What do you wish you could change or fix? List up to five items below. In the column to the far right, as you go through the book and learn about The 7 Deadliest Communication SINs, identify which communication sin that issue falls under.

Communication Challenge	Communication Sin

2 How would you define the hard costs and soft costs of each of these interpersonal communication challenges to you, your work environment, and the company overall?

2 If you were to raise your standard for what you expect from yourself and others, how would you define your expectations in order to have the most effective communication?

The New Standards/Expectation	How It Would Make a Difference

Figure 6

WORKPLACE COMMUNICATION PROBLEM #1

You sit down at your desk after attending a morning meeting, ready to attack your priorities for the day.

Then, unannounced, an employee steps into your office, demanding to speak with you about an issue with a coworker. You listen and tell them, "I'll look into it." Minutes later, the other coworker drops in. You listen and tell them, "I'll look into it."

You may not realize it, but without intending to, you have put yourself in the middle of an employee conflict, with no idea of who's right or wrong. And, it's impacting your work environment and everyone in it.

WORKPLACE COMMUNICATION PROBLEM #2

As you are just getting back to work, your receptionist buzzes with an upset customer on the phone because a promised product or service was delivered late, with a quality below expectations. After speaking with the customer, you realize the cause was an employee failing to follow through. You confront the responsible employee only to hear excuses, deflecting responsibilities, and blaming coworkers. You're frustrated because you don't know who is right, who is wrong, or who is to blame.

So, you chalk it up to "miss" communication! This ambiguity causes you to set it aside to figure it out when you have time. Despite the best of intentions, you never get to it. It's not your fault, because the next simmering fire is waiting for you.

WORKPLACE COMMUNICATION PROBLEM #3

An employee whom you have asked three times in three months to be more punctual getting to work on time is late again. You're frustrated with this employee, and think, *He's not listening. I'm tired of nagging. He needs to step up, take ownership and accountability of his job, or else.* But, the "or else" never comes.

WORKPLACE COMMUNICATION PROBLEM #4

It's annual performance review time. If your workplace is like most, these conversations typically involve the employee's view of their performance being much better than your view of their performance. You've probably noticed these performance review conversations create more disappointment, negativity, and gossip that lead to distrust between you and your team members (and between the employees themselves). The performance review process is causing more problems than it solves.

SOLVING THE 4 WORKPLACE COMMUNICATION PROBLEMS

Each of the four Workplace Communication Problems you read about have the same cause—one or more of The 7 Deadliest Communication Sins, and a complacency that has set in—causing everyone to accept a lower standard of communication in the workplace for one of three reasons:

1. A lack of awareness of the communication sin
2. A lack of consistent practice of the appropriate communication skill
3. A consistent toleration of others in your environment committing this communication sin

PART II.

RAISING THE BAR ON WORKPLACE RESULTS - BREAKING THROUGH THE 3 PRIMARY COMMUNICATION SINS

"Pattern recognition is the ability to see the generic and lasting patterns that underpin localized and ephemeral data, and which form the unseen framework around which lasting success is built."

— Lew McKeown, *Predictable Success*[1]

Standing at the front of a small conference room, I asked ten non-profit CEOs the question I always ask:

"In which areas of your company is communication causing you the biggest challenges and frustrations?"

1. McKeown, Lew. "Pattern Recognition And The Business Of Thinking." *Predictable Success*. December 23, 2011. http://www.predictablesuccess.com/blog/pattern-recognition-and-the-business-of-thinking-2/.

The answers I normally receive are rarely self-reflective.

This time, though, these leaders surprised me with their responses.

They recognized the problem with *their own* communication.

The first three CEOs in succession told me, in one form or another, their biggest personal communication challenge was giving feedback to their employees.

At times after they had delegated tasks that had not been done according to their expectations, these CEOs had found it challenging to give their employees constructive feedback. They realized they had gotten what they deserved, because when they had originally delegated or trained their employee for the task, the CEO had not provided enough specific information for them to even finish the job according to their expectations.

This realization–that it was *their* fault–caused them to either give feedback that was less-than candid, wishy-washy, or that beat around the bush.

Their other approach was to not address it at all–at least in the moment–allowing poor fulfillment of the job to perpetuate until things would become intolerable.

Then they would address the problem directly and candidly in specific terms, much to the dismay of their team member, who felt embarrassed they'd been doing something wrong for weeks or months.

Think about this.

Three CEOs of small organizations in my regional community agreed this dynamic was the primary problem with communication in their organization.

I appreciated the humility and vulnerability they showed in a room of peers.

After that session, I began to ask other small business owners or CEOs about this dynamic. I asked still others in management roles at small companies. They, too, felt this communication dynamic was something they experienced.

A pattern had emerged. I recognized the pattern. Now I could do something about it.

This was the genesis of what I call The Poor Performance Perpetuation Spiral (See Figure 7).

The spiral is a conglomeration of The 3 Primary Communication Sins: Lack of Specificity, Lack of Immediacy, Urgency, and Promptness, and Lack of Directness & Candor. Although those three communication sins make up The Poor Performance Perpetuation Spiral, they also stand by themselves, impacting individual and organizational communication in their own way, which will also be discussed in their own chapters.

The communication sins that make up The Poor Performance Perpetuation Spiral are labeled The 3 Primary Communication Sins because of their global impact on organizations. As you experience these three in the ensuing pages, you will come to realize the overarching impact they have on organizational performance, driven by the interpersonal communication habits and tendencies of those within the organization.

Poor Performance Perpetuation Spiral

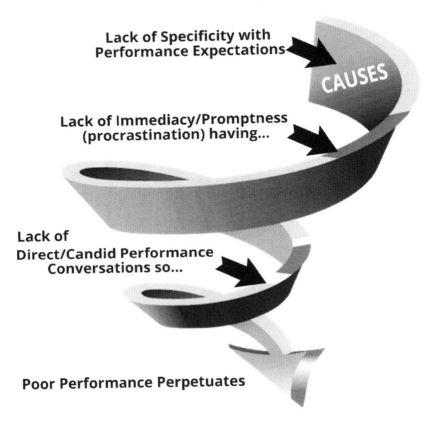

Lack of Specificity with Performance Expectations

CAUSES

Lack of Immediacy/Promptness (procrastination) having...

Lack of Direct/Candid Performance Conversations so...

Poor Performance Perpetuates

Figure 7

The other four communication sins you will read about in Part III impact on a more localized, individual relationship level, affecting the level of trust between two or more individuals. But these four are not as closely related to individual and organizational performance as The 3 Primary Communication Sins.

CHAPTER 3.

LACK OF SPECIFICITY

"Specificity creates clarity. Without clarity, we walk around the block to get next door. We don't know where to focus. We can't agree. We talk more than we act. We measure the wrong things. Specificity creates clarity and clarity creates speed."

— Ann Latham, *The Clarity Papers*[1]

The best job of my career was sometimes the most frustrating.

It seemed like no matter how well I performed, it was never good enough.

In 1993, I was the president, general manager and CEO of a minor league professional baseball team in Erie, Pennsylvania, when we were recruited by a community in New York about 75 miles north of the City.

This was virgin territory for minor league baseball. The community was in need of a shot in the arm of economic and emotional development, and our team provided it. What's more, the site for

---

1. Ann Latham, e-mail message to Skip Weisman, January 16, 2018.

the community's new stadium exemplified the real estate dictum of "location, location, location."

It was the perfect storm to create an unbelievably successful baseball franchise.

We were successful beyond our imagination.

Over the first four seasons, we sold out 92 consecutive home games. We cut off season ticket sales at 1,500 people so we could have seats available to sell smaller ticket packages and at individual games, which gave us a season ticket waiting list of more than 500.

When it came time for individual game tickets to go on sale, we had people camping in our stadium parking lot for days.

It was like I had died and gone to minor league baseball operator heaven.

Year after year over my eight years, we increased revenue and profits.

Yet, when it came time for our year-end review, and having conversations with my boss–the principal owner of the team–it seemed as if it wasn't enough.

Each year, he would ask me to submit a budget. I did, and he would approve it with minor tweaks.

Each year, we would meet or surpass our budgeted goals. Then, the year-end conversation would end not with kudos and congratulations, but comments that made us feel like we could have done better. Often, he would compare our performance to other teams in our organization, highlighting their accomplishments, but never offered what he thought about our team, how we specifically had fallen short, or how we specifically could improve.

Then, it came time to put together the next year's budget, and we'd go through the same dance.

Never did we have conversations around specific revenue or profit expectations on the front end.

What I submitted was typically approved. I always tried to push beyond what we had achieved the year before, and maybe that was all I needed to do to keep my boss happy. But, when it came to review time, it still seemed like we had failed to achieve his expectations.

When I asked for more specificity around his expectations for our year's financial performance, I always got more generalities.

***

"Despite employee claims that it was largely due to personality differences or individual incompetence, we uncovered information that proved that –in most instances- those weren't the primary culprits. In fact, teams in conflict had much higher levels of ambiguity in three categories of work: their team's goals, roles and procedures."

Cy Wakeman – Forbes Magazine[2]

***

The profit-sharing bonus checks (which were significant) were nice. Some verbal praise and specific positive commentary on our performance would also have been helpful.

The lack of specificity around performance expectations was frustrating, because there was nothing for us to measure our performance against, except the prior year's numbers. It was great,

2. Cy Wakeman, "The No. 1 Source Of Workplace Conflict, And How To Avoid It," *Forbes*, June 22, 2015, https://www.forbes.com/sites/cywakeman/2015/06/22/the-1-source-of-workplace-conflict-and-how-to-avoid-it/#2cd7cfcf3b86.

but just not enough for our staff—we always looked for the approval from our boss, which was always inadequate.

This is one way Lack of Specificity starts The Poor Performance Perpetuation Spiral. Although we didn't suffer from poor performance in the scenario I experienced, we never knew how much better we could have, or should have, performed.

CONFLICT RESOLUTION BY CONFLICT AVOIDANCE THE RIGHT WAY

The Three Causes of Interpersonal Conflict

Avoid these and you'll go a long way towards avoiding conflict with coworkers (and family members):

1. **Questioning others' intentions**: When you question someone's intentions, you are indicating you know what the other person was thinking and why. You are projecting their motivations, which is pure speculation. Imagine if someone questioned your intentions?
2. **Unmet expectations**: If someone expects a certain outcome that doesn't manifest, and you were involved in the situation and had influence on the outcome in some way, this is going to cause an upset that will have to be addressed and could cause conflict. Invest time on the front end of the situation to communicate with specificity to gain clarity around expected outcomes and agree on what is realistic to expect.
3. **Violating someone's rules**: We all have rules for how things have to be and the way we want them to be. Often, we don't even know what our rules are until

someone violates them and causes an upset. Be clear on situations where you have rules for the way things have to be, have to be done, or people have to act, etc. Communicate them to others involved so your rules are not violated. Ask about any "rules" others have so you do not violate theirs.

MISSING THE GAME

When someone has success at a young age, it often makes that person overconfident and cocky.

I was thrust into a senior leadership role at a young age–CEO by 26–and in my second year, that overconfidence cost me significant embarrassment and bonus money.

It was all due to this communication sin–Lack of Specificity.

In August, 1987 (my second year as CEO of my first minor league professional baseball team in Greensboro, N.C.), our team was scheduled to play a road game in Gastonia, a two-hour drive away. For short trips like that, we would commute down and back to avoid the extra cost of putting the players in a hotel room overnight.

In our league, and in most minor league baseball leagues at the time, nearly all teams played a day-game on Sundays through mid-June, and as the summer weather heated up, they moved their Sunday home games to night starting times.

When our team played on the road on the weekends, it became a rare in-season off-day for our staff.

I scheduled the bus to pick the team up at our stadium locker room at 3:30 p.m. for the two-hour drive to Gastonia. That would get us there in enough time for the team to stretch and take infield practice before the game.

Because that Sunday was a day off for me, I scheduled a full day of golf, and hit the links by 8 a.m. We played 36 holes, and got off the course around 5 p.m. I was home by six.

When I arrived back at my apartment, there were 34 messages on my answering machine.

That's weird, I thought. *That's an awful lot of messages.*

I hit play.

It was the owner of the Gastonia baseball team, calling every few minutes between 12 noon and 2:30 p.m. with increasing levels of concern and distress.

Game time had been 2:30 p.m., not 7:30 p.m., as I had assumed.

We missed the game.

ninth when Mike Easier led off with a home run, his second, and Wash- ... run homer, his 31st, in the third.

Hornets arrive too late; Gastonia does not wait

A mix-up in starting times caused the scheduled South Atlantic League baseball game between Greensboro and Gastonia to be canceled Sunday.

The Hornets, scheduled to play a game beginning at 2:30 p.m. Sunday in Gastonia, did not leave Greensboro until 3:15 p.m. because the Hornets thought the game was scheduled for a 7:30 p.m. start. When the Hornets arrived, Gastonia had already left the park.

"We hadn't played an afternoon game since June, and we just made a mistake and assumed it was a night game," said Hornets' general manager Skip Weisman. "I talked to John Moss (SAL President) Sunday night, and he said to try and play a doubleheader at Gastonia tonight or

either at our place Tuesday."

Weisman said he spoke with Gastonia president Jack Farnsworth Sunday evening, and Farnsworth wanted to check with his team's manager and farm system director before agreeing on a makeup date. Weisman added the teams will probably play two games against Gastonia in Greensboro on Tuesday night.

The Hornets, 18-44 in the Northern Division of the SAL in the second half of the split season, trail fifth-place Gastonia by six games. The two teams are scheduled to play tonight in Gastonia at 7:30 p.m., before Greensboro returns home on Tuesday and Wednesday against Gastonia in its final two home appearances of the season.

Molitor From B4

sas City's Bret Saberhagen leading   ning. Robin Yount and Glenn

Figure 8

As far as I know, it may have been the only time in the history of professional sports a team did not show up for a game on the road, at least barring a travel disaster like a plane, train, or bus accident.

No, this happened due to a good old lack of specificity.

I had made an assumption about the game time. I hadn't confirmed with the Gastonia general manager. I hadn't checked with our field manager. Therefore, he hadn't asked me to confirm the game time–he, too, had assumed I had it right.

In this instance, I suffered from a lack of specificity around the game time. I didn't confirm–I assumed.

My assumption even made the news (See Figure 8).[3]

The old adage is, "when you assume, you make an 'ass' out of 'u' and 'me.'" This was true on that day. It caused our team, our league, and me tremendous embarrassment. It cost me significantly in the pocketbook, as my boss required me to pay the fine assessed to the team.

It was an expensive lesson.

THE EPIDEMIC

The white paper I published in 2011 on this topic opened with this communication sin at the top of the list, for a reason that hasn't changed over the ensuing years. It could probably be at the top of the list of all communication issues, ever since the cavemen drew on their cave walls.

Once I became aware of the Lack of Specificity in communication, it's been almost impossible for me not to notice.

This communication sin surfaces in every walk of life, and in many different forms. Improve it, and you will improve your communication effectiveness by 50% immediately, starting today!

---

3. "Hornets Arrive Too Late; Gastonia Does Not Wait," *Greensboro News and Record* (Greensboro, NC), Aug. 24, 1987.

BEWARE OF UNIVERSALS, ABSOLUTES, AND EXAGGERATIONS

Universals/Absolutes:

Universals are another common communication habit that can get people into trouble. You've heard them, and you've said them. These are words like "all," "none," "always," "never," "everyone," and "no one."

Those words are used in phrases I bet you've experienced:

- "You always/never do this."

- "They all say that."

- "Everyone does these things."

Exaggerations:

Similar to universals and absolutes, exaggerations can get you into trouble. I love when people say things like:

- "It's happened a million times!"

- "He's killing me!"

- "She is the absolute worst."

People are too quick to throw these phrases out when trying to make a strong point. They come from an emotional place and create an emotional reaction in others. Sometimes, they are used purposely to generate an emotional reaction, for good or bad reasons. They are rarely helpful and need to be evaluated against reality so we can communicate in more effective, realistic ways to build higher levels of trust and respect with others.

MIXED MESSAGES

While interviewing staff members for one of my first small business consulting clients, I learned most everyone felt their boss, Jerry–the owner of the company–was communicating in a way that sent mixed messages.

Those mixed messages caused confusion in the work environment about what was most important and what company priorities were.

For example, the owner spoke often about "safety" being a core value of the company, and it was important for the technicians out in the field to have a "safety first" focus.

Yet when it came time for the technicians to get their vehicles serviced and regular maintenance performed, the owner would try to cut corners. He would ask if they could get away with just having the front brakes serviced, or only the rear tires replaced when the auto service professional recommended all four be done.

It gave the company's service technicians a sense "safety first" was meant only for customers on job sites, and not for them. This really negatively impacted the employees' motivation, morale and commitment to the company.

Mixed messages are a big problem in companies large and small. This type of communication causes stress, strife, lost productivity, and conflict in the work environment.

It comes in different forms. The most common mixed messages result from:

- Constantly changing priorities
- Company leaders violating–and enabling others to violate–the professed company values

- Marketing messages that are inconsistent and confusing for the public, requiring the company personnel to deliver high levels of customer service to make up for confusing the public.

Here are a few funny examples of the last point:

Figure 9   Figure 10

The sign on the left (Figure 9) was posted in a municipal down-town parking garage. A friend–who is a member of the credit union–parked in one of these parking spaces to do business downtown. She was parked there for a couple of hours and came back to find a ticket on her windshield.

She complained to the credit union, and was told the sign was intended to mean parking was only good for the times during which someone was doing business in the credit union.

Within seven days, we noticed the disclaimer on the bottom of the sign was added (Figure 10).

Figure 11

While walking down Main St. in Beacon, New York, on our way to dinner, my wife and I passed the sign above (Figure 11).

It's obvious the store was open, but the sign outside reads, "Coming Soon." I read it to mean the business was "coming soon," yet it looked like they were already open for business. It was very confusing.

My guess is there may have been a new product promotion on the chalkboard for something "coming soon" that had been erased, and no one noticed the irony.

Figure 12   Figure 13

As a third example, my wife and I saw the sign on the left (Figure 12) while pulling into a large convenient mart to get gas for our car.

My wife read this as we could get five subs for three dollars, or 60 cents per sub. What a great deal!

I believe they were trying to convey five different types of subs were available for three dollars each.

Later, I noticed a new sign (Figure 13), and they had added an "each." I must not have been the only one to call them out on their confusing language!

I wonder how many people walked out of QuickCheck with five subs to feed their entire gang for just $3 until these signs were changed?

These different signs are all designed to attract customers or to serve existing customers, and you can probably see how those initial signs caused confusion–and a confused mind doesn't buy.

Having to change these signs after they are produced en masse comes with unnecessary costs in time and money. That time could be better spent on generating positive return on investment, instead of correcting mistakes.

WEAK LANGUAGE

At a networking event a few years ago, a woman I knew from the community sidled up to me and said, "Skip, I'd like to refer you to my boss. We're having some communication issues in our company I think you can help with. Would it be okay if I introduced you to Joe via email?"

"Certainly," I said.

The next Tuesday afternoon, I received that email–sent to both Joe and me. In it, she asked if Joe would be open to speaking with me about the issues she was experiencing around communication in her work environment.

About 48 hours later, on Thursday afternoon, Joe responded. His email read, "I'd be happy to speak with Skip–have him call me anytime."

Because I was on my computer or smartphone almost all the time (as you will learn if you ever engage me for coaching, consulting, or speaking) I replied to Joe within an hour with the following message:

"Joe, thank you for your interest in speaking. How is Friday at 10:00 a.m. or Monday at 2:00 p.m. for an introductory phone conversation?"

He wrote back within 15 minutes, "No, Skip, please call me late Tuesday afternoon. I'm taking Friday and Monday off."

Now, you may be thinking the same thing I was thinking in that moment.

I began to type an email reply: "Joe, what happened to 'anytime'?"

Have you ever received an email that caused an emotional reaction within you? One that triggered an immediate, snippy response from you, which either began to slowly erode, or worse, instantly destroyed your existing or potential relationship?

Have you ever *sent* that reactive, relationship-damaging email? I hope not.

I didn't. I caught myself in the moment, thought better of it, and wrote instead, "Joe, okay, that's great; enjoy your long weekend. I'll call you 4:00 p.m. Tuesday afternoon."

About an hour later, I received a response from Joe, again, which read, "Skip, please call me a little after 5:00 p.m. on Tuesday, as that is when I'll have time to speak with you on my way home in the car."

Again, I began typing an email: "Joe, what happened to 'anytime'?" Again, I thought better of it. I deleted it, and wrote a conciliatory email confirming I would call at that time.

Tuesday came. Five p.m. came. I waited for a few minutes after 5:00 p.m., as he had suggested. When I called him, his phone rang three or four times, and then his voicemail picked up.

It took us another ten days of voicemail tag and emails to finally have that initial conversation.

What happened? What caused this egregious waste of time and energy? A lack of specificity!

"Anytime" is a non-specific word, isn't it? It means basically nothing. There is no substance to "anytime." In my mind, "anytime" means "no time."

It is just one of hundreds of non-specific words and phrases that get thrown around as if they mean something. But, they don't.

Here are some others you may have experienced and even used:

- As soon as possible (ASAP)
- When you can get to it
- When you have a moment
- By close of business (COB)
- At your convenience
- Let's talk next week
- I'm almost done
- Maybe later
- I'll touch base with you
- I'll get back to you on that
- Whenever
- We should get together

What other non-specific words or phrases do you hear that require you be a mind-reader, or cause you extra work, or waste your time?

RIGHT TIME/WRONG PLACE (OR VICE-VERSA)

As a professional speaker and small business coach, I work out of my home. Frequently, I will also schedule appointments with prospective clients or business associates at local restaurants (my preferred office away from my office is Panera Bread).

Within about 15 miles there are three Panera locations. If the person with whom I'm scheduled to meet is even just a few minutes late, I get anxious, thinking I may have gotten the location, or the time for our meeting, wrong. Most of the time, my anxiety is proven unnecessary, as my colleague walks through the door moments later, or texts me they are running late.

If we did get it wrong, as happens from time to time, it wouldn't be the first time. It probably wouldn't be the last.

This is the simple way a Lack of Specificity could play out. One side or the other fails to capture the specificity needed from the scheduling conversation to get it right.

Basic as it may be, it can impact your relationships, credibility, and trust with others if these situations occur more than once. One time is excusable, two times is a concern, and three times is a pattern that causes me to question your intent, commitment, and sincerity as the relationship slowly erodes.

SETTING PERFORMANCE & BEHAVIOR EXPECTATIONS

Imagine it's time for you to write your direct report's annual performance review. You sit down and go through the evaluation form, marking the "poor," "fair," "satisfactory," "good," or "excellent," boxes for each performance category.

When you reach the area of the form to explain your evaluation, you are at a loss for examples, or for any specific reason, beyond the last 30-45 days.

So you give nonspecific feedback and a generic total score–one above-average but below-exceptional–because you want to be fair, but give them too high of a score and they might expect a raise.

You submit the document to your report, and prepare to sit down for the performance review with them. But the conversation becomes either a stressful monologue as you lecture at them, or simply a contentious dialogue.

The generic feedback flows into generic improvement goals for the next performance period, and the conversations tend to devolve, year after year, into a scene from the Bill Murray movie *Groundhog Day*.

Another version of this occurs at the very beginning of an employee's relationship. Typically, it begins with non-specific job performance, attitude, and behavior expectations. This non-specific criteria makes it very difficult for a manager or supervisor to provide specific feedback, constructive or positive, because there is no foundation on which to have a conversation that has any substance, references, or meaning.

These types of conversations around performance, attitudes, and behavior on the job devolve into debates and hurt feelings caused by misunderstandings, confusion, and mixed messages.

Earlier, I spoke about The Poor Performance Perpetuation Spiral. These performance management scenarios are the genesis of this downward spiral (see Figure 7), which keeps individuals and organizations from progressing beyond the status quo.

Poor Performance Perpetuation Spiral

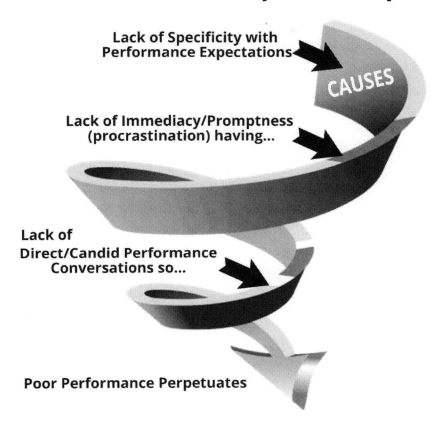

Lack of Specificity with Performance Expectations

CAUSES

Lack of Immediacy/Promptness (procrastination) having...

Lack of Direct/Candid Performance Conversations so...

Poor Performance Perpetuates

Figure 7

This forces small business leaders, managers, and supervisors–as well as their employees–away from improving both individual and organizational performance. This ultimately causes company leaders and frontline employees to tolerate their poor performance, creating low levels of employee morale, employee engagement, and motivation.

This communication dynamic leads to low productivity in the workplace, which costs real dollars and cents. Audience members in my keynotes and seminars, and company leaders in strategic work sessions, tell me this dynamic and other low-level, ineffective communication is wasting at least one hour per day, per employee.

What is it costing your company? What is the average salary and benefits package? If you were to multiply those two figures by the number of work days per year, what is your annual cost of poor communication in your work environment?

Additionally, when poor communication begins to infiltrate a workplace culture in the way described above, it often also leads to higher-than-desired turnover. This turnover comes with high out-of-pocket costs that also get lost in the financial performance of the company and can be significant.

The No. 1 Source of Workplace Conflict, and How to Avoid It

3 Communication Issues That Lead To Conflict:

- Unmet expectations
- Rule violations
- Questioning intentions

Lack of Clarity Leads to Unmet Expectations, Questioning Intentions, and Rules Violations.

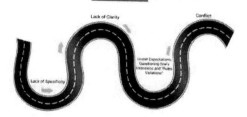

1. Lack of Specificity leads to Lack of Clarity
2. Lack of Clarity leads to Unmet Expectations
3. Unmet Expectations, Questioning One's Intentions, and "Rules Violations" leads to Conflict

Example:

1. A spouse calls home to say to his/her partner, "I have to work late tonight and I'll be home later than usual." (They don't specify how long or why they have to stay late, and the spouse on the receiving end accepts the message without pushing for greater specificity on the time frame).

2. This gives the receiving spouse a "Lack of Clarity" about when their partner will be home after work. They don't know when to expect them, so they are left confused and frustrated, not knowing whether to wait to eat dinner or eat dinner by themselves.

3. The spouse comes home three hours later than usual, 9 p.m. instead of 6 p.m. Because three hours was not specified, the waiting spouse began to disaster -fantasize about what was happening. They had placed the expectation that "working late" meant one hour, so the three hours caused unmet expectations. Their "rule" of family dinner has also been violated, and they began questioning their spouse's intentions, thinking that work is more important than family for their partner, and maybe they are even having an affair with a workplace colleague.

Figure 14

SOLUTIONS TO PRACTICE

This may seem like the most obvious answer of all time: Communicate with greater specificity.

Done. Let's move on, right?

Not so fast.

There is, and must be, nuance to communicating with specificity.

Here are a couple of things that will help you get it right:

1. Know your audience.

Too much specificity is condescending in the realm of providing instructions, or explaining what is necessary or required. For example, if my wife reminds me to make sure I lock the front door when we leave together for the day, she doesn't need to explain to me how to do it; she assumes I know the "how."

Often, the "how" is irrelevant to the "what" of the outcome. Give people the end requirements, be specific about what it should look like, and let them develop their own "how." You can debrief their "how" after the project is complete as a learning opportunity.

To avoid seeming condescending to a veteran employee, you could frame your language at the outset with a simple statement, such as, "You probably already know this, so I'm just making sure so you/we get it right."

If they're a new employee, we tend to forget we know more than they do in certain contexts and leave out pertinent information. You can use similar language speaking with them, such as, "I'm not sure if you know this yet," or, "You may or may not know this, so I just want to make sure..."

Framing conversations and directions in this way shows you respect the individual while also reinforcing the need for specificity that leads to clarity.

2. Avoid the "Law of Familiarity."

Often, the longer we've been in a relationship with someone, or the longer the person has been on the job in our organization, the easier it is for us to get lazy in our communication and assume they will know what we mean.

Even though we may have the best of intentions, we may inadvertently leave some details out. Or, we may leave things out purposefully for efficiency's sake, believing the person "should know these things by now," but they don't.

Be sure to communicate with specificity, even with the people you know, otherwise, they may feel like you've thrown them under the bus, purposely set them up for failure, or didn't care enough to communicate better.

3. Understand more words do not equal more specificity.

You probably know people who tell an entire backstory to explain something, and you get lost in all their words, unsure of their point.

Practice being as succinct as possible. Apply your high school teacher's advice on essay-writing: "Long enough to make your argument, and short enough to be interesting."

Follow the SBAR (Situation, Background, Assessment, and Results) model for structuring your communication. Include these four most important points–no more, no less. (For more information on the SBAR model, see *Chapter 9: Lack of Focused Attention*).

4. Be aware of when you do or don't have enough information from others to perform the expected action successfully.

If you ever find yourself confused or lacking needed information, do not leave the scene of the conversation, or return to it immediately upon recognizing the problem. You don't want to be left guessing or mind-reading.

Lack of Specificity is Communication Sin #1 for a reason. It is the most important, but, with simple adjustments, you can dramatically improve your communication effectiveness and build trust with those around you.

ACTION STEPS

HIGHER PRODUCTIVITY

1. Set a higher standard for yourself and your team.

Commit to specificity in your language, whether about expectations, feedback, meetings, or deadlines. This will raise the standard for performance expectations.

Change your voicemail to reflect this commitment. Instead of, "I will return your call as soon as possible," promise a specific time frame, such as "within three hours," as I do, or something similar. Whatever time you identify, commit, and do it!

2. Be Diligent With Deadlines

Expect specific language on deadlines, both in giving and receiving requests.

Frame your language around this example: "I can get this back to you by 5 p.m. next Friday, April 17. If anything comes up before then that will affect that delivery date, I will get in touch to let you know what's going on, and provide an updated delivery date or discuss other alternatives with you."

3. Sell the Specificity

Often, we are apprehensive of providing greater specificity or asking for it from others because it makes us feel too pushy and aggressive.

To overcome this fear, simply add these four words to your request: "so that (you/we/I) can."

For example: "Please get me the report draft by Tuesday at 5:00 p.m., so that we can have enough time to review and revise it before submitting it by Friday's deadline." Or, "So that we can review and revise the report before submitting it by Friday's deadline, please get me the report draft by Tuesday at 5:00 p.m."

CHAPTER 3 ASSESSMENT QUESTIONS

LACK OF SPECIFICITY

On a scale of 1-10 (1=no knowledge or awareness, and 10=I've been fully aware for a long time), grade yourself on the level of awareness you had on the importance of specificity in your interpersonal communication:

1 2 3 4 5 6 7 8 9 10

On a scale of 1-10 (1=not very consistent or diligent, and 10=very consistent and diligent), grade yourself on your consistency and diligence in ensuring all the interpersonal communication interactions you initiate have the right amount of specificity:

1 2 3 4 5 6 7 8 9 10

On a scale of 1-10 (1=not committed at all, and 10=very committed), grade yourself on your commitment to ensuring all of the interpersonal communication interactions others bring to you have the right amount of specificity (meaning you expect, encourage, and reinforce a safe environment for communicating with specificity and ask for it when you recognize it is missing):

1 2 3 4 5 6 7 8 9 10

In which areas of specificity are you committed to raising your communication standard?

1._____

2._____

3._____

RESOURCES

- *The Clarity Papers: The Executive's Guide to Clear Thinking and Better, Faster Results* by Ann Latham

- *The Influencing Option: The Art of Building a Profit Culture in Business* by Libby Wagner

CHAPTER 4.

LACK OF IMMEDIACY, URGENCY, & PROMPTNESS

"An average person who develops the habit of setting clear priorities and getting important tasks completed quickly will run circles around a genius who talks a lot and makes wonderful plans but gets very little done."

–Brian Tracy, *Eat That Frog*[1]

I was sitting at my stadium office desk one afternoon, mid-way through my baseball executive career. It was right after the end of the season, and things were slowing down around the office.

Suddenly, I heard two loud voices having a spirited discussion. I put my head down and kept focusing on my work.

As I sat, the voices got louder, and louder, and louder.

As the person most responsible for the behavior and performance of those employees, as well as the overall work environment, I knew I had to do something. Yet, I felt glued to my chair, suffering from an affliction you may be familiar with.

It's called CAPD: Confrontation Avoidance Personality Disorder.

---

1. Brian Tracy, *Eat That Frog* (San Francisco: Berrett-Koehler Publishers, Inc., 2002), 2.

You may know someone who suffers from CAPD. It may even be yourself.

Finally, I mustered the gumption–though still with a lot of trepidation–to hustle down the hallway to see what was going on.

I stepped between the two employees just before it got physical. It was seconds away from becoming a really serious issue.

The two employees were sent to neutral offices, and I finally dealt with an issue that had been brewing for five months.

My avoidance came with significant costs.

First, we lost both those key employees and had to figure out how to replace them.

Second, it came with personal costs: one of the two people involved was my wife. Eighteen months later, we were divorced.

To her credit, she had been trying to do the right thing. She felt this other employee had been taking advantage of me and I had been avoiding the issue.

She was right.

So, she stepped up to confront an issue *I* should have faced months earlier.

This is CAPD at its worst, and it causes this second communication sin: Lack of Immediacy, Urgency, and Promptness.

This may be the #1 most universal problem known to humanity. It is probably the cause of most people's misery, disdain, and self-immolation. You may not have heard it put in these terms, but something you may be more familiar with as a term and a habit is... procrastination!

Confrontation Avoidance Personality Disorder

Although not an official diagnosis, there are many, many people who shy away from what could be confrontational interactions. This is communication procrastination, as the avoidance comes with real costs, emotionally, financially, and in terms of interpersonal relationships.

If you suffer from CAPD, I would recommend getting help. Use what you learn in this book and look for other resources to help you understand how to address difficult situations head-on in a prompt, direct, and respectful manner. It takes time, practice, and courage to break through CAPD, and when you do, you will build much higher levels of self-esteem, self-confidence, and self-worth while building higher trust relationships with those around you.

Think about it. Are you experiencing, or have experienced in the past, any of these thoughts, feelings, or actions?

1. Waiting on someone to get something to you that you've asked for, and they agreed to provide, but it is way past the expected delivery time frame
2. Wishing others had a greater sense of urgency
3. Putting off a conversation you need to have with someone
4. Holding off on reconnecting with someone you've agreed to get something for, because you don't have everything they have requested and you don't want to give them something that's incomplete

All of those scenarios fall under this communication sin, which amounts to "communication procrastination."

When I bring this up in my keynotes and seminars, people cower, as they feel they've been "found out." Their secret little procrastination habit has been exposed.

They shouldn't feel ashamed, because procrastination may be the one thing all human beings have in common, beyond birth, death, and our biological human needs.

Within three years of starting my coaching practice in 2002, I even noticed this same communication procrastination pattern in my clients, who were very successful small business owners with companies between $1 and $10 million in annual revenues.

This communication sin, as with all the others, comes in many forms. It is also a major player in The Poor Performance Perpetuation Spiral.

As you review the sample situations below, notice which ones cause you the biggest problems.

You can assess the severity against the three levels of procrastination impact (the 3D Level of Severity):

- **Distracting**

  Procrastination hangs over your head, sapping focus and energy. The only person impacted is you, but it does cause you anxiety, stress, and concern as it perpetuates, and key items on your to-do list are never completed.

- **Debilitating**

  Your procrastination habit begins to negatively impact results and slowly erodes relationships.

- **Destructive**

  You can destroy yourself, your business, and your relationships. Deadlines are missed, appointments continually rescheduled, and people lose their ability to count on you. Trust is destroyed, and the relationships you need begin to slip away.

THE DECISION "BLACK HOLE"

If there is one complaint I hear most often from employees during my culture assessments when I start any client initiative, it's that their boss takes their idea for organizational improvement, agrees with it, and puts it on some list—where it's never heard from again.

It's the one sure-fire way to have employees stop caring about their workplace: they share valid ideas, and their superiors fail to act on them.

In one of these interviews with an employee (from the company in *Chapter 3: Mixed Messages*) I heard from a service technician, Stan, who was in the field driving a van every day to provide services on construction sites. He was frustrated by how long he had to wait to get approval to have his vehicle serviced.

He was responsible for maintaining the vehicle on a regular schedule and he would go to his boss, the owner of the small business, Jerry, with the estimate.

Then, he would wait—days, sometimes weeks—for the approval.

In the meantime, Stan would be concerned about the vehicle's safety, as it would be past due for new tires or brakes.

This was especially demotivating and demoralizing for Stan and his colleagues in the service department, because the company owner had always professed his biggest concern, and the most important company value, was "safety."

His procrastination on vehicle service was inconsistent with his proclamation that safety was his primary value.

At another client initiative an employee, Betty, in charge of sales and customer service for a small manufacturing company, told me she would bring suggestions for operational improvements to her boss, the company owner Jay. He would always be open to listening and would capture the ideas on a spreadsheet to show he found value in the idea. Jay had the best of intentions for delving further into the concept and exploring its potential.

But Betty would never hear about it again as the owner, with the best of intentions for taking the operational improvement idea to the next step, would move on to the next thing.

When I first met with Jay, he very proudly showed me his idea spreadsheet. Then, he confessed with embarrassment and frustration he had never done anything with most of the ideas.

Despite the best of intentions, small business owners still struggle with making decisions and taking action on a variety of issues occurring in their work environment, including ideas their employees bring to them for business improvement and issues their employees ask for help with.

It's costing not only their business's time, energy, and money, but also morale and motivation in their work environment.

Procrastination = Fear

If you suffer from CAPD and Communication Procrastination, it will be helpful for you to understand that for every issue on which you procrastinate, there is a fear behind it. Identify those situations that challenge you the most, and then assess the fear causing it.

Once you come to grips with the fear behind your communication procrastination, you can then start to strategize how to fight it. Remember, 90-95% of what you are disaster-fantasizing about, in reality, will never come close to what your imagination is cooking up.

DELIVERING BAD NEWS

In the weeks after the terrorist attacks of 9/11, when I first started my coaching practice, the economy and the financial markets were challenging at best.

Many of my initial clients were financial advisors, whom I coached mostly on goal-setting, focus, and accountability.

It was not a good time to be a financial advisor in the U.S. The dot.com bubble burst, followed by the economic fallout from the 9/11 attacks, and the financial markets plummeted in value.

The difference between the successful financial advisors in those years and those who lost a lot of their client base had little to nothing to do with the devaluation of their clients' investment portfolios. All client portfolios had dropped in value. Instead, it had everything to do with how proactively the financial advisor communicated with their clients.

In other words, if two financial advisors each had a client with a similarly diversified and valued portfolio—which presumably would have lost similar value—the difference between whether a client stayed with that advisor or not was primarily determined by when and how often their advisor communicated with them, projected confidence that they had their eye on their portfolio, and discussed mitigation strategies with them.

The advisors who procrastinated on reaching out to their clients for fear of delivering bad news, or of hearing their clients' concerns about the bad news in the media and seeing their investments fall, were the ones who lost a significant number of their clients and investments to another advisor.

The moral of the story here is, get ahead of bad news and communicate with whoever needs to hear the bad news as proactively as possible.

Even if you don't have any strategies to address the bad news when you call, it won't matter. The call is to simply inform them you're aware and on top of the issue, and you will get back in touch with them at a particular date and time to explore where to go next.

THE BEHAVIOR/PERFORMANCE CHANGE CONVERSATION

When we get to this point in the keynote or seminar, and I ask the audience to raise their hand if, "you need to have a conversation with someone and you've been putting it off." About one-third of the participants raise their hand.

I always ask the follow-up question, "Why are you putting off that conversation?"

Most of the answers I hear are, "It's a difficult conversation."

And they're right, to a point.

It's only difficult to give someone feedback on their behaviors or performance for three reasons:

1. You don't have a high-trust relationship
2. You haven't set and agreed on behavior and performance expectations at the very beginning of the relationship or project
3. You've had a similar conversation in the past, but the person reacted negatively, making it difficult for you to have a conversation in that moment, and you don't want to experience the stress of that situation again (note that this issue probably has its genesis in the two previous reasons)

This is where this communication sin comes into The Poor Performance Perpetuation Spiral. As we continue to put off the conversation, it becomes increasingly difficult to talk about the issue.

Conversations of this ilk rarely, if ever, get easier as time goes by. Therefore, it is vital to address these behavior and performance issues at *the first most appropriate time.*

You may be thinking, though, "Well, Skip, 'the first most appropriate time' is not specific and is committing Communication Sin #1: Lack of Specificity."

You would be correct.

In this regard, it is impossible for me to be specific because your response timing is related to and impacted by environmental factors. As a guideline, I would suggest all behavior and performance issues be addressed within 48 hours to ensure the situation is fresh in everyone's mind.

If you think the conversation is difficult now, wait three weeks and see what response you get. What typically happens is, when the conversation finally does take place, the language is too soft and not direct or candid enough to be effective, and the poor attitudes, behavior, and performance perpetuates.

The sooner you address the issue, the easier it is to be direct and candid, and because the facts are clearer, you reduce the risk of a negative, defensive, and deflective reaction.

REQUEST RATIONALIZATION

Suppose a colleague or co-worker has committed to fulfill a request for you. Fulfilling this request is going to take some time: they may need to gather information, do some research, and connect with others for more details.

The agreed upon deadline is tomorrow. You haven't heard from your colleague, but you're hoping they're working on it and will be in touch to deliver on time.

Tomorrow comes, and you don't hear from them. You wait three more days, then you call them to see what's going on.

They don't answer, so you leave a message. Three more days go by, and you still haven't received a return call.

You call again two days later, and they say, "I'm so sorry! I'm working on it, and I almost have everything you asked for. I'm still waiting for a call back from one last resource."

I call these situations "request rationalizations," because the person rationalizes, "Since I don't have all the information the person requested, I will just wait till I have it all; then I'll get back in touch."

Meanwhile, you are left waiting, wondering, and hoping your request is on their to-do list and is getting done.

Instead, when we find ourselves in these situations, what we should do is proactively stay in touch and provide status updates along the way.

If we apply greater specificity, we can overcome "request rationalization." This could sound like, "I know you need this by next Friday, and if I hit any snags or roadblocks, I will be in touch prior to update you. If you don't hear from me, you can expect I will deliver it on time."

Once a roadblock occurs, or the deadline approaches and you only have a portion of the request complete, let them know. Give them a status update, and ask if they want the partial information or can wait for the entire package.

This will build high levels of trust and will show you in the best light, instead of damaging your reputation as you avoid calls and cause others to have to chase you down for the tasks you've committed to.

SOLUTIONS TO PRACTICE

TO COMMUNICATE WITH GREATER IMMEDIACY, URGENCY, AND PROMPTNESS:

1. When people bring you ideas and suggestions, avoid the "black hole" by giving them the courtesy of a specific, prompt response. Commit to a time frame for a decision. This specificity will both provide clarity to the situation and help to manage expectations. When that time comes, send them one of two answers:

- "Yes, we can, and here's how and when."
- "No, because..." and give a valid business reason.

If you can't make a decision in that time frame, give them a status update by the agreed deadline and create a new, specific deadline for a decision. Set the standard so that you will hold yourself accountable to your commitments.

2. Create check-ins for status updates on commitments you've made with others in case you can't fulfill the request on time. Be proactive in your outreach to provide the updates.

3. Communicate with greater specificity about expectations for deadline delivery, as well as behavior and performance. Then, be relentlessly committed to fulfilling that expectation.

4. Deliver bad news at the first most appropriate time, which should be no more than 48 hours after its occurrence. The more proactive you are, the more likely you are to build a trusting relationship, instead of slowly eroding or destroying it.

Changing your communication in these ways is the key to building high-trust relationships with others. As that high-trust relationship develops, they will know you have their best interests in mind and you always operate and communicate with the best of intentions. This will make having any future "difficult conversations" much, much, easier.

ACTION STEPS

1. Using the provided worksheet (Figure 15) identify and list up to three communications you need to make or conversations you need to have that you've been putting off.
2. Identify your fear associated with each communication or conversation.
3. Assess your procrastination based on the 3D Level of Severity. Is it Distracting, Debilitating, or Destructive?
4. Identify your rationale for choosing your 3D Level of Severity score.
5. For each of the three communications you identified in #1, plan your first step to move that conversation towards resolution. Do you need to send an email to schedule an appointment? Make a phone call? Check your calendar for a specific time you are free? Commit to a set deadline to take that specific next step. Then do it–no excuses.

Action Steps Exercise for **Chapter 4, Communication Sin #2 − A Lack of Immediacy, Urgency, & Promptness**

Your Procrastinated Communication	Fear (What is the fear causing the procrastination? What are you most afraid of that is preventing you from taking action?)	3D Severity Level (Identify the level of severity: 1) A Distraction, 2) Debilitating, 3) Destructive.	3D Severity Level Reasoning (What is your rationale for your 3D Level score?)	1st Step to Resolution (What is your first next step to resolve this issue before it goes any further?)

Figure 15

CHAPTER 4 ASSESSMENT QUESTIONS:

LACK OF IMMEDIACY, URGENCY, & PROMPTNESS

On a scale of 1-10 (1 = no knowledge or awareness, and 10 = I've been fully aware for a long time), grade yourself on the level of awareness you have on the importance of communicating with immediacy, urgency, and promptness, aka "at the first most appropriate time":

1 2 3 4 5 6 7 8 9 10

On a scale of 1-10 (1 = not very consistent or diligent, and 10 = very consistent and diligent), grade yourself on your consistency and diligence in ensuring all the interpersonal communication interactions that you initiate occur with immediacy, urgency, and promptness, aka "at the first most appropriate time":

1 2 3 4 5 6 7 8 9 10

On a scale of 1-10 (1 = not committed at all, and 10 = very committed), grade yourself on your commitment to ensuring all of the interpersonal communication interactions others bring to you occur with immediacy, urgency, and promptness, aka "at the first most appropriate time" (meaning you expect, encourage, and reinforce a safe environment for communicating at the first most appropriate time, and hold people accountable to it):

1 2 3 4 5 6 7 8 9 10

In which areas of your life can you raise your standard to communicate more often at the first most appropriate time and avoid communication procrastination?

1._____

2._____

3._____

RESOURCES

- *How to Say Anything to Anyone* by Shari Harley
- *Eat That Frog* by Brian Tracy
- *Crucial Conversations* by www.VitalSmarts.com
- *Crucial Confrontations* by www.VitalSmarts.com
- *End Procrastination NOW* by Skip Weisman
  (digital audio training available at
  www.EndProcrastinationNOW.com)

CHAPTER 5.

LACK OF DIRECTNESS & CANDOR

"Most people have been told since they learned to talk some version of 'if you don't have anything nice to say, don't say it at all.' When they become a boss, the very thing they have been taught not to do since they were 18 months old is suddenly their job."

–Kim Scott, *Radical Candor*[1]

It was four months into a nine-month consulting project with a $15 million construction company, and I was sitting in a meeting with the senior project manager and his six construction site supervisors.

During the discussion, I heard one of the site supervisors proclaim, "You have to be careful, you know, because we can get fired for no reason."

I forced my way into the conversation. "Excuse me, Pete, what did you just say?"

He repeated the statement, and I asked, "Where did you get that from?"

---

1. Kim Scott, "What is Radical Candor?" *Radical Candor*, 2018, https://www.radicalcandor.com/about-radical-candor/.

Don, another site supervisor said, "Oh, that was made very clear to us in a memo." The others around the conference table supported Don's story.

"I've been working with you for the last four months," I shot back, "and this is the first I'm hearing about this!"

Don replied, "Oh, this was a few years ago."

"Yes," another site supervisor said. "It was probably six or seven years ago."

I was flabbergasted. The next day, I asked my client, Jack–the company owner–about this memo.

He proceeded to tell me the memo had been recommended by the company's attorney after losing a $50,000 wrongful termination lawsuit brought by a former employee.

He confirmed it was about seven years prior.

Jack then went on a rant. "I can't believe these guys are still holding a grudge over that. No one has come to me to ask about that memo or to complain about it. Everyone knows I have an open door policy and people can come in to talk to me about anything whenever they need to."

I said, "You're joking, right?"

"What do you mean?" he asked.

"Jack," I said, "don't you realize you just basically threatened everyone's job, telling them they could be fired at any time without cause, with that one-size-fits-all memo? Do you really believe someone is going to feel confident enough to come in and confront you about it? You're delusional!"

This is an extreme example of one of the most egregious ways this communication sin, Lack of Directness and Candor, can manifest in a work environment.

It's the reason most "open door" policies don't work.

Jack, in this instance, created an environment where people were afraid to deal with issues directly and candidly with the source. Though some in the company would argue Jack's management style was too direct and candid, it wasn't. His style also committed Communication Sin #6: Lack of Appropriate Tone & Body Language, and could be defined as bullying, stifling any directness and candor in the work environment.

Jack's communication style created a CYA ("cover your ass") mentality among employees, who would go behind their coworkers' backs to inform Jack of others' mistakes so they wouldn't get blamed. They did this because they had learned people who made mistakes, or did things counter to Jack's way, faced his wrath—which was not pretty. I witnessed it firsthand.

Jack's employees had learned through his behavior and communication style that the company's supposedly direct, candid culture was a one-way street. It was Jack's way or the highway, so people kept their ideas, thoughts, and unfortunately, their motivations, to themselves.

It's like what Colonel Nathan R. Jessep (played by Jack Nicholson) said in the 1992 movie *A Few Good Men*: "You can't handle the truth."

Many business leaders do not support direct and candid feedback in these open door, impromptu meetings.

Those who do choose to step through that "open door" are typically committing this communication sin themselves by throwing a co-worker under the bus to their boss instead of going directly to the person who is the problem.

A Better Way to Communicate to Motivate

If I had been Jack's coach when the lawsuit had first occurred, I would have recommended he change his approach to how he managed his employees, rather than send a memo. By doing so, there would be no need to bring the possibility of termination to anyone's attention.

The solution is to have relationships with employees based on high-trust and respect, and that only comes from communicating in a way that builds those type of employee-employer relationships. Once those are developed, employees feel they are treated fairly and are respected and would rarely sue their employer for wrongful termination, because a fair performance management process is followed.

When done correctly, employees understand where they stand, how they are doing on the job, and where they need to improve. One of my colleagues, Libby Wagner, offers a mantra to her students in her training program, Managing for High Performance & Retention: "I do not terminate employees. Employees earn termination through consistent non-performance in the face of overwhelming feedback!"

That's the way to communicate to motivate employees, not through non-direct, passive-aggressive, attorney-recommended, company-wide memos.

THE PROBLEM

If Lack of Specificity is the easiest to fix, and Lack of Immediacy, Urgency & Promptness is the most common human communication habit, then Lack of Directness & Candor may be the most damaging of all for both individual relationships and organizational cultures and work environments.

There are two sides to this coin that make it so challenging to incorporate directness and candor into work environments and interpersonal relationships, yet the most successful people are able to figure out how to do it effectively.

Here's what I mean.

As Kim Scott, author of the book *Radical Candor*, writes,

"Two nearly universal experiences make Radical Candor unnatural. One, most people have been told since they learned to talk some version of "if you don't have anything nice to say, don't say it at all." When they become a boss, the very thing they have been taught not to do since they were 18 months old is suddenly their job.

"Furthermore," Scott continues, "most people, since they got their first job, have been told to be 'professional.' Too often, that's code for leaving your humanity at home. But to build strong relationships, you have to Care Personally. You have to bring your whole self to work."[2]

In my keynotes and workshops on The 7 Deadliest Communication Sins, two comments stand out.

2. Kim Scott, "What is Radical Candor?" *Radical Candor*, 2018, https://www.radicalcandor.com/about-radical-candor/.

First, people often tell me, "I have no problem being direct and candid with people. As a matter of fact, the feedback I get is I'm *too* direct and candid."

Second, many say, "The problem is, most people can't handle direct and candid communication, and that's where all the conflict comes from."

Those are the two sides of the coin.

Imagine the dynamic between these two types of people in a conversation. One is comfortable being direct and candid, and the other doesn't respond well to direct and candid communication, especially when it's directly about them or something they've done.

This could go very badly, couldn't it?

People who do not take this feedback well, and get defensive and deflective, usually have a low self-esteem. In those situations, there is not much that can be done by the communicator, except to examine their communication style and framing and try different approaches.

The highest-performing organizations have a culture where directness and candor are the expectation. Yet, outside of the military and sports–which are very hierarchical environments–few business organizations get this right.

With the right commitment from the top, and the right investment in people, almost any organization can create a candid culture. Building this kind of culture is not easy, however, and requires not only commitment from leaders, but a developed high-trust environment, and intensive communication training and coaching.

Many companies, unfortunately, fail to create this kind of culture. As a result, there are several situations that can occur and undermine any positivity and productivity in their work environment.

Below are typical situations in organizations that lack directness and candor, which all contribute to The Poor Performance Perpetuation Spiral. These issues that need to be dealt with are instead ignored and avoided, often at significant costs to individuals and the organization.

THROWING COWORKERS UNDER THE BUS

When I am brought into companies to improve the way people interact and build a more positive, productive, and profitable company culture, I always hear this phrase from people.

There may be no more damaging behavior in a workplace than when coworkers "throw each other under the bus." Rather than having colleagues who have each others' backs, no one can trust each other.

This environment does not emanate from the employees. It comes from management.

In the workplace, this type of mindset develops from the way managers treat their team members. Their behavior teaches their employees how to react and respond.

Managers who treat people inconsistently based on employee behaviors and job performance (which can be perceived as playing favorites), also contribute to this competitive dynamic. They may also communicate in a way that gives the impression they are favoring some over others.

Jack, the owner of the construction company at the beginning of the chapter, had a personality that fostered this type of workplace.

Employees were so fearful of being called out for doing something wrong or contrary to the owner's desired way of doing things, they would go directly to him and call out their co-workers so they wouldn't get blamed for it first.

In this type of work environment, workers are always looking over their shoulder at who may be watching them. They are also always more concerned with what type of work and how much work their co-workers are doing, distracting themselves from the work they should be doing and being less productive than they need to be.

Employees complain about their co-workers and what they're doing or not doing, and people hear things second- or third-hand, instantly destroying those relationships.

If you've ever wondered how toxic work environments develop, look no further.

AVOIDING THE "ELEPHANT IN THE ROOM"

In the fall of 1992, as I sat at a conference room table in a meeting with my fellow directors of the New York-Penn League of Professional Baseball teams, I was dumbfounded.

I was the new kid on the block, the president of the Erie (Pennsylvania) Sailors, and I had just finished my first season leading the league's Erie franchise, but I wasn't new to a league Board of Directors. It was my 11th season in baseball and my seventh as a team's CEO. So despite being a new kid, I had been around the block a time or two.

Yet in that room, sitting around that conference table, many of the other directors had much more business experience. Actually, most were the principal owners of their teams.

Our main charge in the meeting was to interview and assess the candidates for our next league president. Three candidates were under consideration.

One was the current president Leo Pinckney. He had been president for two terms over the last eight seasons. He was a former baseball writer who brought major league-affiliated baseball to his hometown in the late 1950s, and he was a great custodian of the league and advocate for the sport.

Another, Robert F. Julian, was a lawyer from Utica, New York. He was also a season ticket holder with long-term ties to his local community team, which had played in Utica for decades. At the time, the team was called the Utica Blue Sox.

The third candidate I can't remember 26 years later.

After meeting all three and hearing each presentation, the decision was easy for me.

Robert F. Julian had presence, spoke well, had real substantive ideas, and a legal background with high-level negotiating experience as an attorney. These were the skills and talents we needed the other two simply didn't have.

All candidates left the room, and the league directors began deliberations. Each director had their time to give their opinion on the options.

As we went around the room, all I heard was fluff.

There was no directness and candor. Each director spoke eloquently about the fine men we had as candidates, and we "couldn't go wrong" with anyone we chose.

There was strong advocacy for Leo Pinckney due to his long-time commitment to the New-York Penn League, beginning many years before he had even become league president.

But, there was no directness and candor as to what each person would bring to our league, and how one would be different or better from the other.

All comments were plain vanilla.

In our fourteen-team league, I think I was the 11th to share my thoughts.

I was really glad I was towards the end, though, as it gave me a chance to see how all these successful business people were avoiding the elephant in the room.

So, for one of the first times in my life (I had never been much of an assertive speaker in a public setting before this), I spoke up, and brought the elephant into full view.

"There's no doubt each of these three candidates are nice guys, and all would be qualified to be our league president," I said, "but there are differences. We need to speak about those, which I haven't heard much of up to this point."

"I believe," I continued, "based on what I've heard from each of them, and based on my impressions after personally speaking with each of them, the right person to be our next president is Bob Julian. Here's why…"

Later that morning, Robert F. Julian was voted in as the next league president for the New York-Penn League. He served the league well from 1992-2000. Mr. Julian presided over the transformation of the league in quality and credibility, and was responsible for moving some franchises into newly-renovated stadiums and relocating others into new, state-of-the-art stadiums in larger markets.

Have you ever been in a meeting where important issues need to be addressed, but no one does?

Sometimes, those situations are the result of leaders holding back information. When leaders are less than transparent with what's going on in the workplace, rumors can begin to circulate, and a leader who never addresses these in any credible way simply perpetuates the problem.

The larger the organization, the more ubiquitous and problematic this issue can be.

Avoiding the elephants are the greatest reason for low-trust between management and front line employees, gossip, and low-morale and motivation in a work environment or on a team.

The "invisible" elephants can be found and avoided in virtually every type of setting. It can be in a large conference room in a board of directors meeting, like the story above, or it can be in a performance review conversation between a boss and their subordinate.

It can even be in the holy grail of worthless boss communication strategies: the "open door policy." Most "open door policies" don't work because the entire work environment lacks the trust necessary to have the right conversations and is steeped in a culture of a Lack of Directness and Candor (see The 4 Conversations).

Most all situations that lack directness and candor are fear-based.

In one context, a manager's fear prevents him or her from directly addressing the issues. Often, because they don't have answers to issues that generate from many levels above them, they avoid the subject altogether. Failing to candidly discuss what they do know, though, only causes more distrust.

Another context involves a manager's response to those who do broach the subject. Often, subordinates fear repercussions if they speak up publicly, so no one does. Nor does anyone address it privately with someone who could do something about it. Thus, the gossip mill grows.

In a third context, a business owner fears being direct and candid because it requires more transparency than they are comfortable with. In order to be transparent, sometimes leaders must be vulnerable with the people they lead; this exacerbates uncomfortable feelings, and so the fear of communicating in this manner is often paralyzing.

For one of my clients, this transparency was absolutely necessary for him in order to have any hope of turning around his struggling company. As a result, he learned a valuable lesson.

After my encouragement and coaching convinced him to be totally transparent with the financial situation of the company, his fear of his employees jumping ship because of the weak status melted away quickly. His humility, openness, transparency, and vulnerability paid off as his employees rallied around him and the company, stepping up to better work ethics and attitudes to help turn the company around.

In 18 months, the company's revenue increased 33%, and was back on solid footing.

Leaders need to stop seeing the elephants in the room as things to be feared, and begin seeing them as assets that can bring out the best in the people they need most. Doing so will begin to chip away at a culture steeped in a lack of directness and candor and move on to a path towards a high-trust environment where directness and candor are rewarded.

That's where the real magic happens.

CHAMPION COMMUNICATOR'S POWER TRIAD

The best communicators have the ability to balance these three key factors, which allow them to connect with others and build high levels of trust. People tell me being able to balance these at the highest level is often situational, meaning it is easier depending on who we're speaking with and the emotional state we allow ourselves to get into. Regardless of those two factors, the best communicators use emotional intelligence, empathy, and compassion for others, as well as their communication skills, to maintain the balance.

Most of us still developing this skill typically default to two of the power triad, and have a tendency to shy away from a third. Review the diagram (Figure 16) and be honest with yourself as you evaluate your tendency. Identify the situations and people who cause you to bring certain combinations of these factors to the interaction, and assess what you need to work on to build the balance to become a champion communicator.

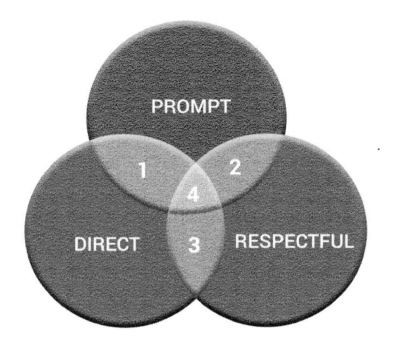

Prompt/Direct =
Too harsh, often with inappropriate
tone/body language, inappropriate environment.

Prompt/Respectful =
Too soft, beating around the bush, non-specific.

Direct/Respectful =
Takes too long to have conversation, loses its
value, plays 'gotcha' too long after fact.

Prompt/Direct/Respectful =
Ideal! Builds trust and gets results.

Figure 16

GLOBAL FEEDBACK ON A LOCALIZED PROBLEM

Have you ever been on a team where there were one or two people gumming up the team's progress? I have.

Too many times, a leader, instead of addressing an issue directly with the individual team member, will call a team meeting and address it in general terms to *everyone* (in situations like this, the perpetrator of the problem becomes "the elephant in the room").

If you've ever experienced this, you know it causes significant discord among team members.

The team members who are performing well become confused, frustrated, and upset they were called into the meeting, when everyone already knows who the problem team members are. This erodes trust within the team, especially between the performing and non-performing team members, as well as the team's confidence in their leader.

To make the situation worse, the one team member with the problem behavior doesn't even get the point they are the problem. They see the meeting as a general rah-rah session, then go on as they were. Nothing changes, and trust and performance continue to decline.

Similarly, a team leader may send out a generic email to all staff members to try to address an issue. This often occurs when one employee has violated a company policy or continually arrives late either for work or meetings.

Instead of the team leader addressing this issue directly with the sole perpetrator, he sends out a blast email to everyone in the organization, whether they are involved or are aware of the issue, or not.

In these circumstances, those who are aware of the situation know what and who the memo is about. Those who are not aware or involved now begin to ask around and delve for gossip about who it might be.

All the while, the true perpetrator remains clueless and thinks the email blast is about someone else or some other situation unrelated to them. Their behavior perpetuates, undermining trust with the individual and throughout the team and overall work environment.

BEATING AROUND THE BUSH

This situation is the one that directly impacts The Poor Performance Perpetuation Spiral and is directly related to the situations described above.

Often, too many organizational leaders don't use direct and candid language during performance conversations. They beat around the bush, speak in generic terms, and are wishy-washy when trying to articulate the attitudes and behaviors that need improvement.

So, as in the generic team meetings explained in Global Feedback on a Localized Problem, these non-direct, non-candid conversations get the same response (an employee who fails to change their approach) and the under-performance continues.

For this situation, there are two steps to break out of The Poor Performance Perpetuation Spiral.

Step one is to recognize there is an individual performance issue that needs to be addressed individually and privately.

If you fail to do this, you will instead fall back into one of several of the situations and sins we've discussed so far, such as dealing with the individual issue generally and publicly in a team meeting, as in Global Feedback on a Localized Problem. Or, you may address it with Communication Sin #2: Lack of Immediacy, Urgency, and Promptness, as you procrastinate or fail to address the issue altogether.

Step two is to use direct and candid language delivered with a respectful tone and body language that addresses the issue head-on at the first most appropriate time (within 48-72 hours max).

It's surprising how basic the non-direct and candid language sometimes can be. For example, in team meetings, you might hear, "we need to have better teamwork," "we dropped the ball on that project," or, "next time, let's make sure we're more focused."

With that type of language, no one is held accountable, and the proverbial "we" points to no one, so no one and nothing changes.

When talking one-on-one with someone in a situation that requires direct and candid feedback or direction, people often use language that beats around the bush and is not as direct and candid as it should be, such as, "you probably should have done...," or "it would have been nice if you could have..." This type of language leaves too much room for misinterpretation by the person receiving the message. Because you aren't specific or direct, they may falsely assume you are offering them flexibility in their approach, which you never meant to offer.

PASSIVE-AGGRESSIVE BEHAVIOR

This may be the most common of all non-direct communication, and comes in a close second to "throwing coworkers under the bus" as the most damaging workplace behavior.

Participants in my workshops and keynotes tell me it is their most frustrating communication style due to the mixed messages it sends and the uncertainty it creates.

Passive-aggressive communication comes in many forms, including:

1. Deliberate procrastination after an agreement
2. Deliberate mistakes couched as accidents
3. Answering only some of a request, or only the first question in a series (often in emails)
4. Making excuses, such as being defensive, deflecting, claiming lack of fairness, or blaming others when offered feedback or constructive criticism
5. Disguising criticism as compliments or sarcasm
6. General sarcasm

To overcome passive-aggressive behavior, it must be addressed directly and candidly as soon as it occurs. This is difficult to do, because addressing it can often cause the perpetrator to become defensive, deflect, or be even more passive-aggressive.

That's okay. Become comfortable with that, because addressing it promptly in this manner is what will get it to stop. It will change people's behavior once they realize they were caught in their passive-aggressive game.

SARCASM

At this point in my keynotes and seminars, I always ask people who are of their sarcastic nature to raise their hands. Many do so with a sense of pride.

Then I follow up with, "Raise your hand if you've been the victim of a hurtful sarcastic comment."

A lot of hands also go in the air, though not as many as the sarcasm perpetrators, and not nearly as assertively. Interestingly, many people raise their hands for both.

Realize the cause of sarcasm is often someone's low self-esteem and insecurities. They are trying to build themselves up by tearing others down.

Depending on frequency and severity, it can border on bullying. Be very careful, because it can devalue even the most trusting, respectful relationships.

Often, in our most intimate relationships, we feel we have the connection to tease and be sarcastic. Many times, you can and it will be fine.

But, you never know when you go over the line until it's too late.

Sarcasm is often hurtful and can either slowly erode the trust in the relationship or instantly destroy it. The reason it is hurtful is shown by its etymology, which is from the Greek word "sarkazein."[3] Sarkazein means "to strip off the flesh." If you've ever been the victim of a hurtful sarcastic comment, you may remember it felt like you had your flesh torn, or at least your ego.

Sarcasm directed at a common situation we are all experiencing can be a good way to release tension and provide a new perspective.

Sarcasm will also be addressed in Communication Sin #6: A Lack of Appropriate Tone & Body Language, as it often comes with a tone that sends a particular message.

THE 4 CONVERSATIONS

Did you know there are only four types of conversations you can engage in? Think about how much easier it will be to have

---

3. *Online Etymology Dictionary, s.v.* "sarcasm," accessed March 23, 2018, https://www.etymonline.com/word/sarcasm.

productive conversations once you learn what they are and can identify which of the four conversations you are having.

The 4 Conversations

Person

		Wrong	Right
Conversation	**Right**	Path or Procrastination *It's Your Choice*	Path of Possibilities *Understanding, Growth & Progress*
	Wrong	BMW (Bitching, Moaning, Whining) *Time & Energy Suckers*	Missed Opportunity *Confidence & Credibility Killers*

Figure 17

WRONG CONVERSATION WITH THE WRONG PERSON (BOTTOM LEFT QUADRANT)

This is usually not a direct and candid conversation. Typically, it involves going behind someone's back to complain (bitch), moan, or whine about them (B.M.W.). Conversations of this kind are usually negative, gossipy, or throw someone under the bus. They can be partially productive, "venting" conversations—which is fine for the very short term—but most people use them for far too long, and become time and energy suckers.

This is a conversation where the person you are speaking to is not someone who can solve your problem or issue (thus, the "wrong" person for this conversation).

RIGHT CONVERSATION WITH THE WRONG PERSON (UPPER LEFT QUADRANT)

This can be a productive conversation if approached the correct way. This means the conversation is about the right topic for a valid reason and purpose.

In this context, the "wrong" person is also defined as someone who cannot directly solve your problem or issue. But, for a short time, they can be a resource for you by becoming the right person in the moment for a very specific role (e.g., being a conduit to the real "right" person, being a sounding board for feedback, role playing, brainstorming, etc.).

At this level, they can also be an enabler by not helping you to move the conversation towards the right person. If this conversation doesn't move toward the right person in short order and is continually being revisited, you are actually slipping back down to the "Wrong Conversation/Wrong Person" quadrant.

Thus the label of "path" or "procrastination." If it moves forward productively towards the right person, it's a path. If you continue to stay in this conversation without forward movement, it becomes procrastination.

WRONG CONVERSATION WITH THE RIGHT PERSON (BOTTOM RIGHT QUADRANT)

This may be the most damaging conversation of all. You can see from the diagram, these kinds of conversations are lost opportunities and can kill credibility and confidence.

Have you ever invested a lot of time and energy to find or get an appointment with the "right" person? It could have been a prospective buyer for your product or service, the owner of a company you wanted to work for, or even someone you found attractive that you wanted to get to know better and start an intimate relationship with.

Imagine you're interested in dating someone. You've brainstormed with your best friend (right conversation with the wrong person) about how to set up a scenario to have this "right conversation with this right person" and the time has come.

You begin with a little small talk to build rapport; things are going well, and you're ready to ask for the date. Then, out of nowhere, your unaware prospective date says, "Hey, you know Jason (your best friend) pretty well don't you? I always thought he was cute and seemed like a nice guy; would you introduce me?"

Boom! All of sudden your "right" person has hijacked this "right" conversation and it immediately becomes the "wrong conversation with the right person."

This becomes a moment of truth, and you either cower or step up.

This is where you need to apply a direct, candid response to get back on track. In this scenario, the best approach is to be direct and candid, and say, "You know, I have no problem doing that, I'd be happy to introduce you to Jason. Before I do, you need to know I was hoping to ask you out on a date because I'd like to get to know you better."

This is the ideal way to reply. Is it the easy way? Not at all. It takes what my high school basketball coach, Ray Newman, would call "intestinal fortitude." But, it is the only way to maintain self-respect and build your self-confidence and self-esteem, by standing up for yourself.

In all situations, you only get one chance to make that great first impression.

Often, you've invested time, energy, and financial or emotional resources to get that opportunity, and you think you're ready. You get in front of that person, start the conversation, and the "right" person hijacks the topic and the focus.

This happens in all types of scenarios, such as:

- Managers trying to give feedback to subordinates who, when approached about something, deflect, make excuses, and blame others.

- Trying to provide empathy to someone who has been hurt in a situation/is going through a difficult time, and the person tells a story about their own experience, making the situation more about them than the person they are trying to show empathy towards.

- Offering ideas in a meeting when someone begins explaining why it won't work or all that is wrong with the idea.

- Telling a story of a great vacation experience and another person picks up on it, and, instead of asking you more about your experience, begins sharing their most recent best vacation.

RIGHT CONVERSATION WITH THE RIGHT PERSON (UPPER RIGHT QUADRANT)

In these conversations, both parties have equal opportunity to express their ideas, opinions, and concerns, and the topic stays on track towards a respectful resolution.

It doesn't mean you get the other person to agree with you or have your request approved. What these conversations do provide are the opportunity to fully express what you need, and you leave the conversation feeling heard and respected, as well as feeling you were able to speak your truth and ask for what you want, need, or feel you deserve.

It's a conversation that builds trust and respect between those directly involved.

These are the conversations we need to make sure we have most often. They are the path of possibility, positivity, progress, and growth.

Understanding the other three conversations will help you see where you spend most of your time and which conversations are the most challenging for you.

SOLUTIONS TO PRACTICE

To start breaking the pattern of this communication sin, practice these approaches:

1. Understand how and why this sin may be the worst of all.

Your lack of directness and candor misleads others. If you don't address a problem, your team or employee may never even realize there is an issue until it's too late.

Athletes are often quoted that they respect coaches who make it clear where they stand. They say, "I may not like what my coach said, or how he feels about my ability to contribute to this team, but at least I know where I stand and what I need to do," whether that be to get back in the lineup, or to stay on the major league roster, etc.

In business, we should treat employees the same.

2. If you're like some of my keynote and workshop participants, and believe you are "too direct and candid," let me tell you what I tell them: I don't believe you can be. Instead, your style may be too assertive, and it is coming across as disrespectful.

I encourage you to get feedback from people you trust to give a direct, candid assessment about your communication style.

Then, explore ways to practice communicating in a more empathetic, compassionate way.

3. Learn how to frame your conversations and structure your language in a way that will encourage others to be open to your direct and candid communication. There are nuanced, yet direct ways to deliver virtually any message (see my training and coaching on *How to Communicate to Influence Up, Down, and All Around*).

4. The only way to put an end to someone else's non-direct, non-candid, passive-aggressive communication is to practice direct, candid communication in reply. Point it out directly to the culprit.

One way to do this safely is to simply point out the discrepancy between what was agreed on and what actually happened.

It would sound something like this: "Jim, last week when we spoke, we both agreed you would pick up this project and get these three things moving forward by today, and thus far I haven't seen any progress on any of them."

Leave it at that, and let them respond.

If they deflect, make excuses, or blame, simply repeat what you said: "I appreciate those challenges, *and* despite those, we agreed you would complete these tasks by today, and so I'd like to revisit that commitment and get a firm date on when I can expect to see results."

From there, though you may sound like a broken record, hold them accountable to their commitment with consistent, firm variations of the statement above.

5. Commit to always going to the source of the issue.

- Never go behind an individual's back to the "wrong person," who cannot resolve the issue (this is gossip and is unhelpful).
- Never communicate generically to a group where an individual is the cause.
- Never send a generic email about an issue. Always have a face-to-face meeting, either individually or with a group to address concerns or problems.

ACTION STEPS

1. Use the worksheet (Figure 18) to identify people in your sphere of influence you need to be more direct and candid with.
2. Write down what you need to speak directly and candidly with them about.
3. Identify the fear that has prevented you from being direct and candid to this point.
4. Schedule a specific time, *within 48-72 hours*, to have this direct conversation, with *only* the person with whom there is an issue.

5. Use what you have written down in #2 to craft your conversation before you have it.
6. Be aware of your tone and body language during your meeting–be direct and candid, but respectful and open to their feedback and communication.

Action Steps Exercise for **for Chapter 5, Communication Sin #3 – A Lack of Immediacy, Urgency, & Promptness**

Person with whom you need to have a direct/ candid conversation	What, specifically, do you need to speak with them about?	What is the fear that has prevented you from being direct and candid up to this point, if any?	Select the first most appropriate time to have the conversation. ____ (no later than 72 hours from now)	Have the conversation and write down how it went & what you learned.

Figure 18

CHAPTER 5 ASSESSMENT QUESTIONS

LACK OF DIRECTNESS & CANDOR

On a scale of 1-10 (1 = no knowledge or awareness, and 10 = I've been fully aware for a long time), grade yourself on the level of awareness you had on the importance of communicating with directness and candor:

1 2 3 4 5 6 7 8 9 10

On a scale of 1-10 (1 = not very consistent or diligent, and 10 = very consistent and diligent), grade yourself on your consistency and diligence ensuring all the interpersonal communication interactions you initiate occur with directness and candor:

1 2 3 4 5 6 7 8 9 10

On a scale of 1-10 (1 = not committed at all, and 10 = very committed), grade yourself on your commitment to ensuring all of the interpersonal communication interactions others bring to you occurs with directness and candor (meaning you expect, encourage, and reinforce a safe environment for directness and candor, and you ask for it when you believe it is not present):

1 2 3 4 5 6 7 8 9 10

What are three areas of your personal and/or professional life where you would gain the biggest benefit when you begin communicating with more directness and candor?

1._____

2._____

3._____

RESOURCES

- *How to Say Anything to Anyone* by Shari Harley

- *Radical Candor* by Kim Scott

- *Crucial Conversations* by www.VitalSmarts.com

- *Crucial Confrontations* by www.VitalSmarts.com

- *How to Communicate to Influence Up, Down, and All Around* by Skip Weisman www.CommunicationPowerForLeaders.com

- In 2016, I created a eleven-minute training video called *The Worst Workplace Behavior: What It Is, Its Causes, Costs, & Cures*, in which I discuss passive-aggressive behavior in more detail to help you deal with it. Email me at Skip@WorkplaceCommunicationExpert.com and I will send you the link to view it.

PART III.

BUILDING A POSITIVE, PRODUCTIVE & CIVIL WORK ENVIRONMENT - OVERCOMING THE PULL OF THE 4 SECONDARY COMMUNICATION SINS

"Communication leads to community, that is, to understanding, intimacy, and mutual valuing."

–Rollo May

Not all communication fulfills Rollo May's claim. The 4 Secondary Communication Sins are the cause.

You will notice, as you read each communication sin, these four also interact with and reinforce each other, showing up in the same communication.

Every communication has the *potential* to do what May, the 20th Century existential psychologist suggests in his quote, but most of our communication falls short.

In my experience, the majority of humans are not seeking "understanding, intimacy and mutual valuing." At least, it doesn't seem so these days, does it?

In Chapter 2, I stated the purpose of communication is to influence and direct the situations, experiences, and results in your life.

Every day, we have dozens to hundreds of interactions with other human beings. Each of those requires some form of communication, and, as you read in Chapter 1, each results in one of three outcomes:

In every communication interaction, you are either building trust and improving the relationship, slowly eroding trust and the relationship, or instantly destroying trust and the relationship.

The odds are not in your favor when you communicate. You have a 67% risk of damaging the relationship with the person with whom you are communicating.

Every day, in your interactions with others, you have the potential to commit one or more of The 4 Secondary Communication Sins. How you choose to communicate within the context of those situations will impact your relationships with others, for better or worse (with a 67% risk of getting it wrong). What you learn in the ensuing chapters will help put the odds back in your favor.

Whether in an organization or a family, the quality of the overall culture of a community is directly related to the quality of the communication between the individuals who belong to it.

The 4 Secondary Communication Sins are just as seriously impacting the quality of your relationships as The 3 Primary Communication Sins. As a matter of fact, one of these four is more likely to instantly destroy trust and relationships than the other three.

As you read through each communication sin, I guarantee they will trigger memories of specific interactions you've had with others, allowing you to notice the impact they've had on you, your reaction and response, and how the relationship was impacted.

CHAPTER 6.

LACK OF RESPECTFUL REBUTTALS

"When you start a sentence with "no," "but," "however," or any variation thereof, no matter how friendly your tone or how many cute mollifying phrases you throw in to acknowledge the other person's feelings, the message to the other person is 'You Are Wrong.'"

–Marshall Goldsmith, *What Got You Here, Won't Get You There*[1]

In the second year of my first CEO position, I noticed an opportunity to increase the revenue for our company.

One of the key areas of revenue for our company was the advertising in our nightly game program, which was printed once for our entire five-month season.

Historically, we had five pages of player profiles, with five players' photos on each page and a short biography and personal data about them. Opposite this page, we would sell a sponsor a full-page ad.

The opportunity I saw was to break up the player pages into smaller increments. Instead of five, we would feature only two

1. Marshall Goldsmith, *What Got You Here Won't Get You There* (New York: Hyperion, 2007), 57-58.

players in on a quarter-page, which opened up two quarter-page sponsorship positions next to each player.

We could go from selling just five premium sponsorship, full-page positions, to 26 player-sponsor positions.

Previously, we had sold the full-page player-sponsorship pages for $1,000 each, generating a total of $5,000.

With my new layout, we could sell 13 player-sponsored pages for $800 each ($400 per sponsored-player, quarter-page ad), doubling our revenue from sponsored pages.

It was a no-brainer.

A few weeks prior to our year-end organizational meetings, I told my boss I wanted time to present my idea. Executives from all six teams in our organization would be attending.

He agreed, and at the appointed time, I made my presentation.

When I was finished, our big boss–the principal owner of the franchise who had started in Nashville, Tennessee, and now spread to six cities in the Southeast U.S.–leaned back in his chair.

He slowly pulled out a big cigar, lit it, took a long drag. He exhaled, blowing smoke into the air above his head, and said, "Skip, that's a great idea, but we don't do it that way in Nashville."

That was the end of the conversation.

He might as well have said, "If we don't do it in Nashville, you won't be doing it in Greensboro, either."

I was devastated.

I couldn't understand how a plan to generate double the revenue, as well as open more premium positions for sponsors to promote their own players, couldn't be a great idea for all involved.

More importantly, though, his statement, "Skip, that's a great idea," confused me.

How could someone say something is a "great idea," and then refuse to implement it? Or, at least not allow one of our cities to implement it on a trial basis, and evaluate from there?

For the rest of the afternoon, I checked out.

I was confused. I continually asked myself, "Did he really think it was a good idea, or was he just blowing cigar smoke to make me feel good?"

I also began feeling a sense of learned helplessness. I had had the organization's best interest in mind, looking at ways we could generate more revenue in a win-win scenario for all, and presented a case everyone thought made sense. Yet, this "great idea" was shot down without a viable explanation or any specificity as to why we couldn't implement it.

Have you ever experienced a "re-BUT-tal" like that?

This communication sin is all about the disingenuous language pattern of using a positive opening statement, followed by a "BUT" to counter and undermine that positive statement.

MY LESSON IN BUTS

While going through my professional development after my divorce, I spent two years immersed in weeklong workshops every 90-120 days with Anthony Robbins.

After one workshop, he offered a follow-up weekend program called *Communication Power.* It was in this program I first learned about the power and the problem of the word "BUT."

Through interactive role play exercises (which are offered at the end of this chapter for you to practice) I learned how hard it was during discussions and debates, to not say "but," "however," or "although," when countering and trying make my point.

With that simple role-play exercise, I learned for the first time how those three words (and other euphemisms, like "now, having said all that...") negate whatever comes before it. I learned it comes across as very disingenuous, causing the other person to stop listening.

Yet, despite our best intentions, it was hard not to use those words in rebuttal. It felt like the "but" was on the tip of my tongue, waiting to come out. That language pattern is a deeply-ingrained communication habit, and is hard to break.

In these types of interactions, you must be very conscious of how you want to phrase your words in a rebuttal to maintain a respectful conversation that moves towards a mutually amenable resolution–and hopefully agreement. (Note: "Agreement" doesn't necessarily have to be the end result, and often cannot be due to irreconcilable differences).

Most importantly, that workshop activity brought back the memory of my boss' rebuttal in the story above, where I was "butted" and had my hard-thought-out idea rejected in front of a room full of peers. Remembering how I felt in that situation helped me to realize how damaging this type of language really is.

A few years later, while reading Marshall Goldsmith's, *What Got You Here Won't Get You There*, I was reminded of the danger of "buts" again.

We must beware the message we communicate when we use this type of language. Goldsmith writes, "It's not, 'I have a different opinion.' It's not, 'Perhaps you are misinformed.' It's not, 'I disagree with you.' It's blatantly and unequivocally, 'What you are saying is wrong, and what I'm saying is right.' Nothing productive can happen after that."

He later adds, "from there, the conversation dissolves into a pointless war. You're no longer communicating. You're both trying to win."[2]

Goldsmith also refers to people who use "cute mollifying phrases" meant to acknowledge and appreciate the other person's feelings, opinions, ideas, etc., (like my boss's phrase "Skip, that's a great idea..."). These phrases provide what seems to be supportive and positive language before they drop the anvil on you.

It's a disingenuous and dangerous language pattern.

Power communicators are aware of this, and do everything in their power to avoid it.

It's not easy.

This language pattern has been ingrained into our vernacular since the early days of our language development as a toddler. Most of the people we're around as we're developing our language skills are unaware of this damaging language pattern, so we pick it up from them and it becomes our default way of communicating.

It is habitual. Meaning, hard to break.

It is slowly eroding your relationships, both consciously and subconsciously.

At the end of this chapter, you'll have the opportunity to practice building a new habit to break this disingenuous language pattern.

2. Marshall Goldsmith, *What Got You Here Won't Get You There* (New York: Hyperion, 2007), 58.

LOSE YOUR BUT

The Lack of Respectful Rebuttals situations you are likely to experience are all very similar, such as:

- Debates–trying to convince someone of your opinion
- Giving someone constructive feedback while trying to protect their feelings
- When responding to objections

That statement my boss used, "Skip, that's a great idea, but…" as I stated earlier, confused me. Did he really think it was a good idea, or not? Since he didn't approve it, he must not have thought it was a great idea, so why did he say that?

Most all rebuttal situations are the same because they involve someone who has something negative to say, they try to begin with a positive statement, and they undermine the positive by using "but," coming across as disingenuous.

Most people have the best of intentions when using this language pattern. They want people to have an open mind and listen to their feedback, ideas, and opinions. They know providing positive, complimentary commentary at the beginning will help, and it does.

Then the "but" comes and undermines everything before it.

Most people tell me they feel deflated when they hear a "but" because they know something contradictory is coming.

Those same people tell me that's when they stop listening.

They believe their partner in the conversation is being disingenuous, they put a wall up because they feel undermined, and so the language slowly erodes the relationship.

You hear these "but" statements more often than you might realize.

Though all rebuttal situations are very similar due to the language pattern, the specific contexts in which these conversations occur are varied, and can appear in virtually any context of your business or personal life.

For example, a manager might be talking to an employee about his ideas, job performance, contributions, efforts on a project, or future opportunities.

For example, a manager might be talking to an employee about his ideas, job performance, contributions, efforts on a project, or future opportunities.

Disrespectful rebuttals in various contexts might sound like this:

- "That's a really great idea, *but*, it would never work in our industry."
- "You did a really great job, *but*, here are some ways you missed the mark and could have done better."
- "I appreciate all the overtime you've been working on this project, *but*, have you noticed how results in these other areas are taking a hit?"
- "That does seem like a great opportunity for you, *but*, it also seems like a distraction from what you should be focusing on."

If you want to build trust with someone, lose the "but."

Instead, substitute the "but" with an "and" to soften the transition.

"And" will keep the other person engaged in the conversation, and you will be able to build on what you truly believe.

With "and" as a transition, you will have to be much more conscious about what you're going to say next. If you use the same language as you would have after the "but," the "and" won't necessarily make your message less negative, and your statement might become more confusing.

Also, a best practice for using the "and" as a transition is to ask a question to keep the engagement going. Rarely in conversations where people use a "but" is there even a thought of wanting to keep the conversation going; it's typically used to shut down the conversation and move on.

Make note of these tips in the examples below:

Example 1:

- "That's a really great idea, but, it would never work in our industry."
- "That's a really great idea, and, it would never work in our industry."

Notice how I included the word "and," but didn't change any of my following words. Did it make my message any more positive? Just using the "and" like this doesn't do much to convey that you see value in the idea.

You are going to need to adjust your language, offer specific reasons, and show real appreciation along with the "and," such as:

- "That's a really great idea, and, I'm concerned it won't work in our industry because…"

Example 2:

- "You did a really great job, but, you missed some things that would have made it better.

- "You did a really great job, and, you missed some things that would have made it better.

There isn't much difference in tone between these two statements. In fact, your message is even more confusing. Here is an even better way to rephrase it:

- "You did a really great job, and, I've noticed some areas you missed that would have made it an even better job. Would you be open to learning about them?"

The respectful rebuttal approach benefits the conversation in several ways:

1. It puts the emphasis on your personal observation, and makes it obvious your evaluation is an *opinion*, not a blanket rejection of the good job you've done.
2. Adding the word "even" reinforces the "good job" opening statement, thus building on it. It is much more likely to keep the person leaning in and listening, as it comes after the "and," instead of a "but."
3. You are either providing a reason for your opinion as in Example 1, or, as in Example 2, you are asking for permission to share with them your personal opinion and observation–if they are open to learning.

Again, because they haven't been shut down and stopped listening after a "but," they will be more likely to be open to continuing the conversation and learning from you because they are more likely to believe you want to be genuinely helpful.

Here are a couple more examples of respectful rebuttals:

- "I appreciate all the overtime you've been working on this project, and I am concerned some results in these other areas may be taking a hit. Would you be open to learning how that may be the case?"

- "That does seem like a great opportunity for you, and it also seems like its a distraction from what you should be focusing on. What do you think?"

CAVEAT

If you don't believe it's a "good idea" or that someone "did a good job," or you don't think "their effort was a good use of time," don't start your sentence with the disingenuous fluff. Doing so is committing Communication Sin #3: Lack of Directness & Candor. In those circumstances, you have two options:

1. Find another context to be positive about. Use the "and" to make your direct, candid point the rebuttal, such as, "I appreciate your effort coming up with that idea, and based on my experience with similar approaches, it's not a idea that will work."

It is also helpful to ask if they'd like to learn what your experience has been. For example, you could add, "Would you be open to learning about my experiences that have led me to this conclusion? I'm happy to explore those with you to see if they're no longer valid."

Remember, most of the time we use "but," is to simply and quickly shut down the conversation and move on. People who have made an effort in certain areas deserve an explanation and reasoning, not just a put-down.

2. Be direct and candid on all fronts. Tell them in a respectful manner, with the right tone, what your opinion is: "Based on our present situation, that's not an idea I'm comfortable looking at right now, and here's why."

Again, the respectful part of the rebuttal is the reasoning for your opinion. People deserve that, and it is something you should want to provide, as you can use it as a learning opportunity and a way to bring people along to your way of thinking.

The good part about this approach is it can spark discussion and exploration that will lead to building trust and the relationship which, at the end of the day, is what we should want most.

CREATING EMPATHY WITH "AND"

People debate all the time whether on everyday details or expansive emotionally-charged issues. Debates often cause hurt feelings, and can also either slowly erode or instantly destroy relationships.

Using the strategy of "and" instead of "but" can diffuse the emotional intensity many conversations devolve into.

Remember, if someone hears a "but," "however," or "although," they are more likely to stop listening, shut down, or begin to feel they are not being heard.

Because using "but" does not project empathy and compassion, it has the potential to raise the emotional intensity of the conversation and undermine a positive experience that could build understanding.

This plays out daily in the current political discourse in family, friend, and workplace discussions.

If we want to have a substantive conversation and have any

chance of keeping the discourse respectful and productive, this is one strategy that can help.

The key is to *want* to find common ground, and be truly supportive and appreciative of another's opinions and ideas.

Some good phrases to use in these situations are:

- "I appreciate what you are saying and why you may feel this way..."
- "I understand what you are saying and why you are saying it..."
- "I agree with much of what you are saying and why you are saying it..."

Most of the time, the next word is a "but." You now know the "but" will cause the other to shut down and stop listening, though.

In these debate situations, where people may feel personal credibility is at stake, the "but" has the potential to provoke ire in people, causing them to get defensive or snap into attack mode–not good for building the relationship in a positive manner.

If you shift to using "and," there is a greater likelihood they will be more open to hearing your opinion, and more so if you use powerful transition language to clearly communicate what you are about to express is solely your experience and opinion, such as:

- "I appreciate what you are saying and why you may feel this way, and what my experience has been is..."
- "I understand what you are saying and why you are saying it, and what I've seen in similar situations..."
- "I agree with much of what you are saying, why you are saying it, and what I've learned over the years is..."

I'm hopeful this chapter has given you insights into the power of language and how the syntax of your words, and the specific words you choose to use, can make a difference in your ability to connect and build a trusting relationship with other people, be they your bosses, subordinates, peers, or significant others.

As with all other communication strategies in this book, these strategies are not guaranteed to work in every situation, because there are other human beings in the situations with you. Remember, they have just as much influence on the outcome of a communication as you.

I *do* guarantee practicing and applying more respectful rebuttals will add to your communication ability and will help put the odds of success for influencing and directing the situations, experiences, and results in your life, back in your favor.

FINAL POINT

This is going to feel uncomfortable at first. It is also going to feel like you can't make your point strong enough and you are committing Communication Sin #3 by not being direct and candid. This is only because it is a new skill you're building.

When you learn to transition with "and," and use the suggested phrases to follow the "and," you will be able to make your point strong enough and be direct and candid, while also respecting the other person you're working to build the relationship with.

I know this to be a fact, because for the last ten years I've had the privilege of working with a colleague on some projects. Sandy is a former counselor who had a private practice before getting into organizational development consulting.

In 10 years of collaborating and partnering with her on a half-dozen projects, I cannot remember her ever using "but," "however," or "although," in a conversation with me or any of our clients.

Sandy is a very conscious communicator, and it is a pleasure to speak and work with her. She is tremendously successful, and by practicing the "respectful rebuttals" strategy suggested in this chapter, you will build the habits that will allow others to feel empowered and positive in your presence, too, even in the most challenging conversations.

BUT-BUSTING PRACTICE

EXERCISE #1

For the next week, track every "but," "however," and "although" you hear each day. Write the word every time you hear it in a notebook or journal. This is better than counting with stick figures, as it will reinforce the word you're hearing in your mind. Make note of the person who said it and the context it was used in.

At the end of the week, you will be amazed by how often this language is used.

For bonus points, add "no" to the list. Marshall Goldsmith does this in coaching his clients and it adds a powerful dimension to your learning by seeing how frequently "no" comes up.

EXERCISE #2

Find a partner to play with and pick a nebulous, relatively non-emotional topic to debate, such as:

- **Best sport:** baseball, football, basketball, hockey, soccer, rugby, tennis
- **Favorite sports team:** you pick 'em
- **Favorite beverage:** coffee, tea, water, sparkling water, soda (ex: Coke vs. Pepsi)
- **Favorite Vacation:** warm weather or cold weather
- **Favorite Season:** winter, spring, summer, or fall
- **Best Fast Food Restaurant:** McDonald's, Burger King, Wendy's, Popeyes, Bojangles'
- **Beer:** Domestic brands, international brands, local microbrews

The actual topic doesn't matter, just make sure you each have an affinity for one option so you can speak to the benefits of your selection.

One person starts the conversation with a positive, selling statement about why they like their choice and why it is obviously better.

The partner, the second person to speak, provides their rebuttal using one of these three statements:

1. I understand what you are saying, and…
2. I appreciate what you are telling me, and…
3. I agree with you, and…

It is important to stick to only these statements when rebutting your partner.

Go back and forth at least 5 times rebutting each other and notice what happens.

This practice activity is the best to help make you a much more conscious communicator.

CAVEAT

Like building any new skill, this is going to be uncomfortable and not feel right. It's going to feel like you are not able to make your point strong enough. When you practice this enough and become more adept at crafting your language in this manner, this approach will make you a much more powerful communicator. You will begin to notice people staying more engaged in the conversation as well as more actively listening to you, allowing you to better bring challenging conversations to equitable resolution, or, at a minimum, a level of understanding that maintains a trusting, respectful relationship.

SOLUTIONS TO PRACTICE

You may be confusing people, or worse, harming relationships and trust through how you respond to them. Here are a few solutions:

1. Identify the contexts in which you use the words "but," "however," "although," etc. in your day.
2. Beware of using "cute, mollifying language," in an attempt to sugar-coat your disrespectful rebuttal. If what they have to say is worthy of praise, be authentic and specific–this will help to transform your rebuttal into a respectful one.
3. Practice finding common ground and empathizing with people when you have discussions with them.
4. Remember, the purpose of this chapter is not to eliminate "but," "however," and "although" from your vernacular. In most instances, they are fine to use. They are only a problem during conversations involving differences of opinion, debates, or giving someone candid/direct feedback–when you may be tempted to offer positive fluff at the outset of your statement to soften the blow of the real message you want to deliver.
5. See the other chapter exercises for more "but"-busting practice!

ACTION STEPS

RESPECTFUL FEEDBACK

When someone comes to you with an idea:

1. Listen carefully to what they have to say.
2. Even if you disagree, try to find common ground with them and view the issue from their point of view.
3. Provide authentic, specific praise if appropriate.

4. Phrase your respectful feedback with an "and" instead of a "but," and follow with your specific reasoning.
5. Keep the conversation going. Ask a question, or invite their feedback. Make sure they know you hear and respect their opinion, and that you are open to any future ideas they may have.

CHAPTER 6 ASSESSMENT QUESTIONS

LACK OF RESPECTFUL REBUTTALS

On a scale of 1-10 (1 = no knowledge or awareness, and 10 = I've been fully aware for a long time), grade yourself on the level of awareness you had on the importance of communicating without using "BUT" or its other euphemisms in a conversation:

1 2 3 4 5 6 7 8 9 10

On a scale of 1-10 (1 = not very consistent or diligent, and 10 = very consistent and diligent), grade yourself on your consistency and diligence ensuring all the interpersonal communication interactions that you initiate are respectful rebuttals:

1 2 3 4 5 6 7 8 9 10

On a scale of 1-10 (1 = not committed at all, and 10 = very committed), grade yourself on your commitment to ensuring all of the interpersonal communication interactions others bring to you use respectful rebuttals (meaning you expect, encourage, and reinforce communicating with respectful rebuttals and hold people accountable to communicating in this manner):

1 2 3 4 5 6 7 8 9 10

What are three areas of your personal and/or professional life where you would gain the biggest benefit using respectful rebuttals?

1._____

2._____

3._____

RESOURCES

- *What Got You Here Won't Get You There* by Marshall Goldsmith

CHAPTER 7.

LACK OF DESIRABLE BEHAVIORS

"One of the most distinctive characteristics of a good influencer is that this person is able to translate what she doesn't want into what she does."

–Libby Wagner, *The Influencing Option*[1]

In 1997, I began studying at an elite yoga academy where the core fundamentals were taught. This was back before yoga studios were on every corner of every town in America.

After 10 years, the school relocated to an area that made it impractical for me to continue attending, which forced me to find other outlets for exercise.

For convenience's sake, I settled for my local fitness center.

In one of my last classes, the instructor took us through a series of poses.

While in the Warrior 1 Pose (see Figure 19), she told us, "Try not to have your front knee straighten."

---

1. Libby Wagner, *The Influencing Option* (UK: Global Professional Publishing, November 11, 2010), 83.

Figure 19

Immediately, my leg began to straighten, and my body rose. I focused my mind on sinking down into the pose again, with my leg fully bent so my thigh and shin were at a 90-degree angle.

To maintain balance between both sides of our bodies, we made sure we did the same exercise a second time on the other side.

This time through the pose, the instructor said, "Make sure your front knee is over your front ankle, and your thigh is parallel to the ground."

With those instructions, I felt my body sink naturally deeper into the pose.

The difference between the yoga teachers' first set of instructions and the second, is what this communication sin represents.

The first set of instructions had focused my mind and body on the opposite behavior and movement the teacher wanted from us. For me and most of my classmates, the instructions had the opposite of the intended result.

The second set of instructions had focused our mind and body on the desired behavior, and allowed everyone to succeed in settling in to the right body position to attain maximum benefit from the pose.

Even though this communication sin example comes from a yoga class, it has huge implications in your world, too.

You experience this communication sin frequently in your personal and professional life.

If you're a parent of a child between two and twenty-two, it is causing your biggest frustrations.

If you're leading a team of people and have direct reports, it is causing negative feelings in your work relationships, and is negatively impacting the results you can achieve through and with others.

This communication sin is the Lack of Desirable Behaviors, which means you're focusing on the things people are doing wrong, communicating about what people are doing wrong, and rarely reinforce what people are doing right.

Some specific examples you may be familiar with include:

1. Don't forget the report is due on Friday.
2. Stop coming late to work.
3. Don't miss the deadline on Tuesday.
4. Stop interrupting me.
5. Don't come in the house with your dirty shoes on.
6. Stop slamming the door.
7. Don't tailgate when you're driving.

Often, when you use that kind of language, the behaviors continue. There are two primary reasons for this.

First, the language is non-specific.

This lack of specificity causes a cycle of trial and error. People may change their behavior according to your instruction, but because you have only told them what you don't like and what you want them not to do, they may still get it wrong. This causes you to give them further direction that often is also non-specific, and the cycle continues.

This ongoing trial and error erodes trust. They feel like they are constantly having their wrist slapped, and develop a sense of "learned helplessness," stop listening, and the relationship is significantly damaged.

The concept of learned helplessness is very important for leaders to understand because they often, unknowingly, create a work environment that causes feelings of learned helplessness in their team.

According to the Encyclopedia Britannica, Psychologist Martin Seligman first used the phrase "learned helplessness" to describe the effect continuous and unavoidable negative stimuli had on the dogs he performed his conditioning experiments on. Because there was nothing they could do to escape the negative stimuli, the dogs would eventually give up trying to avoid it–they believed they had no control.[2]

The same thing can happen to people, even at work. Employees stop thinking for themselves and trying to do things on their own because they believe they are just going to be criticized and corrected. They only do the minimum for their job, and always wait for direction from their superiors.

This creates an interesting workplace dynamic, as one of the biggest complaints I hear from small business leaders is employ-

2. *Encyclopedia Britannica Online, s.v.* "learned helplessness," accessed Feb. 27, 2018, https://www.britannica.com/science/learned-helplessness.

ees don't take initiative on the job and are not proactive enough getting things done.

The argument could be made that the leaders committing this communication sin are the cause of one of their biggest employee performance frustrations.

When I first started speaking on the topic of this book, audience members in my sessions would tell me they definitely saw how overcoming this communication sin had value for their personal lives, especially if they were parents of children between the ages of two and 22. However, they didn't see much application in the business work environment.

Not long after I began hearing that feedback, though, I was invited in to provide an in-depth, four-week training on *Overcoming The 7 Deadliest Communication Sins* to 30 middle managers working at the largest CPA firm in our region with just under 100 total employees.

During one of the sessions, as we began exploring this communication sin, a young lady named Samantha raised her hand. She told me and her coworkers, "Last week, when I went to the partner I report to to ask him a question, he responded with, 'Stop asking me the same questions over and over.'"

"What did you do after that?" I asked.

"I walked out of his office, pretty upset he wasn't willing to help me, and I went to ask someone else."

"So," I asked, "how did you feel about that? What have you done since?"

"I felt embarrassed, ashamed, and not very supported. And honestly," she said, "I've been avoiding dealing with him ever since."

"If he's your boss, that doesn't sound like a good long-term solution."

Samantha agreed.

The next day, I called this firm's partner who oversaw Samantha and asked him about it.

"Yes," he said, "I've become pretty frustrated with Samantha, as she has a tendency to continually ask for help on items she should be assimilating into her level of work, and she should be coming to me with higher level questions by now."

"Well," I told him, "how you responded to her in that moment and the type of language you used has upset her and turned her away from coming to you again. I think her confidence is shaken, and so she's afraid of coming to you to ask any type of question now, and I'm confident that was not your intent."

He agreed.

In just that one incident, Samantha had embarked on a path towards learned helplessness.

I coached Samantha's partner on this communication and suggested better language for him to use next time by focusing on giving feedback that would encourage Samantha (or any other of his direct reports) to look to improve her approach.

The better way to address this would be with language such as, "Samantha, I'm wondering if you are aware that this is basically the same question you asked me last week about X client. Do you remember? I'm concerned you aren't assimilating the answers I'm giving you into your knowledge bank, so you can learn what you need to become more self-sufficient at this level of work.

"What I'd like for you to do when we speak about your questions is bring a notebook and write down the client situation, the tax code component, and my suggestion for the best ways to approach the situation. This will do a couple of things: first, it will help you remember it because you are writing it down in addition to listening; second, it will provide you with a point of reference for future, similar client situations; and third, you will become more familiar with this level of client situation, allowing you to come to me with more advanced questions so I can help you grow in your career. Is that something you would be open to working with me on?"

Notice this approach. It begins by more softly showing Samantha she was bringing the same question to him on multiple occasions, and it made that point very clear. It gave her an opportunity to let the partner know she didn't recognize the similarity in the situations so she could get help from him in that regard, if necessary. And finally, it gave her specific instructions on how she should approach her learning and development moving forward, and created an expectation for her future behavior.

This approach leaves little room for misunderstanding or the need for mind-reading. It also provides Samantha with specific, actionable steps to take control of her own development—steps her boss would be willing to help her with. This gives Samantha more confidence that her boss cares about her and doesn't want to be dismissive, as he seemed originally.

These types of conversations happen often in a work environment. Now that you are aware of them, you too will start noticing them.

The second reason for little or no change when you use language focused on the undesirable behavior, is the power of your mind to focus.

Where you focus goes, energy flows, and the subject of that focus grows. Whatever you pay attention to is what you will notice more of, and it will seem you are getting more of it.

You may or may not actually be getting more of it, but it certainly seems that way because of your focus on it.

This is how your mind is designed to work. It's actually a part of your brain called the Reticular Activating System: the "part of the reticular formation in the brainstem that plays a central role in bodily and behavioral alertness."[3]

As with most brain functions, it's complicated in how it works. The simple explanation is one of its functions is to regulate sleep, states of wake, and alertness.

Have you ever noticed once you become aware of a concept or a product, or even a word you just learned the meaning of, you begin seeing it more frequently?

Many years ago, my mother's health started to fail and she was forced to go on dialysis for kidney failure. I helped my father and mother with the initial search for a dialysis center she could go to near their home.

Upon returning to my home about three hours away, I immediately noticed a dialysis center less than a mile from my home. It had been there for years, but only now, because dialysis was an important part of my life, did I become a aware of it.

A more common example of this is if you've ever purchased a new car that is a different make, model and color from any other you've previously owned.

In those situations, you've never given much thought to this new type of car before, and haven't noticed it on the road very often. Almost immediately after driving your new car off the dealer's lot, however, you begin noticing similar cars just like yours in make, model and color.

3. *Dictionary.com, s.v.* "reticular activating system," accessed Feb. 27, 2018, http://www.dictionary.com/browse/reticular-activating-system?s=t.

Do other people on that day also decide to purchase that same type of car? Probably not; it's just that this make, model and color of car is now important to you, it is now something you identify with, and your mind now begins noticing things that are important to you.

Here is another example, related to leading employees in small business. Remember my former client, Jack, from *Chapter 5: Lack of Directness and Candor*? As you might imagine from that story, Jack was a stickler for details.

When he would go around on construction sites to inspect the work, he made note of everything on the site either done wrong, still needed to be done, or was a safety hazard he felt was unaddressed by the site supervisor. Jack would capture it on his notepad, and while on the site in public, with other people around, would confront the site supervisor with his laundry list of what was wrong, incomplete, or hazardous.

His employees on construction projects would feel highly stressed when he came onsite, worried about all the undesirable things about the work they were doing.

I got this feedback from the employees, and I confronted Jack about it. He said, "If the work is done right, and done well, I don't have to worry about it. My concern is all the things I have to worry about that can cost us money or are safety issues. That has to be my focus."

I asked him, "How do you think that constant focus on all they aren't doing right or haven't gotten to yet affects your construction site team?"

"I don't care how it affects them," he said. "They have no attention to detail. I have to treat them like children."

"Well," I said, "for the next month, when you to go inspect a site and are on the site, you are to only praise people. Consciously look for things you like and make twice as many notes of what you like than what you don't like. Make note of the undesirable things you need to remind people about, and keep it to yourself until later in the day."

He looked at me, concerned, and I said, "Then, later in the day, call the site supervisor so it is a private phone conversation between the two of you. You are to praise him again for all the good things you noticed, and respectfully ask him if he is aware of the undesirable things you noticed."

This activity changed how Jack saw his construction sites, and began to change how he saw his people. He began focusing at least as much on the desirable behaviors, actions, and contributions of his employees as he did on the undesirable things that needed to be fixed so he could ensure they were taken care of.

Attitudes and morale in the company began to change, and stress in the environment was significantly reduced.

CONCLUSION

To recap, if you communicate by mostly focusing on the undesirable behaviors of others and do not offer any suggestions for the alternate desirable behaviors, you will be caught in continual trial-and-error mode, getting a different undesirable behavior each time.

Because it is the wrong behavior, you are going to correct it. Do this often enough, though, and you risk damaging the relationship.

This is why in parenting and in leading employees, people feel like they are continually doing it wrong, getting their hand slapped, and can't get anything right in someone else's eyes. Not only is this demoralizing, it can also produce that feeling of learned helplessness in your children or employees. This is not your intent, and gives you the opposite result of you're looking for and need.

The other important factor is to understand that communicating only the undesirable behavior is not future-focused. Remember, the undesirable behavior you experienced from the other person took place in the past. They cannot change the past; they (and you) can only change future behavior. Continuing to harp on that undesirable behavior keeps both of you immersed in the past.

Identifying, articulating, and having a conversation on what successful behavior should look like the next time gives you and the other individual an opportunity to chart a different future. You can influence the future, so when you focus your attention on that future desirable behavior, both you and your child, your employee, or your coworker, will have something specific to measure against. You will know it when you see it. You can't measure or prove a "don't," a "stop," or a "didn't."

Switching your language to the desirable behavior will also reinforce your use of specificity. As you build new language habits, not only will you be able to overcome Lack of Desirable Behaviors, but Lack of Specificity, as well.

SOLUTIONS TO PRACTICE

There are two things you can do to overcome this tendency in order to create a more positive and productive work environment.

1. Decide you are going to be focused on reinforcing the positive, desirable behavior you want people to engage in.

When you see it, say it. If you want to get more of the desirable behavior, you need to let people know that's what you want to see more of.

2. Begin communicating the desirable behavior you want to see that you are not currently seeing.

Instead of telling people what not to do or to stop doing something every time you witness an undesirable behavior, immediately identify the alternative desirable behavior. Define, with specificity, what you want them to do instead.

Shift your language like my yoga instructor did. Don't tell me, "Don't straighten your front knee." Tell me to keep my front knee over my front ankle, and my thigh parallel to the ground.

Using this kind of language is important for two reasons:

- First, human beings cannot *not* think of something. Try not to think of a pink elephant. In order to not think of a pink elephant, though, you have to first think of it. Only then can you move away from that thought to something else. In this way, focusing your language on the undesirable behavior reinforces the undesirable behavior in the mind of the person with whom you are communicating.

- Second, it is easier and more efficient if we focus on what we want instead of what we don't want.

ACTION STEPS

DESIRABLE BEHAVIOR

Create a worksheet (or use the one below) with two columns: "Undesirable Behaviors" and "Desirable Behaviors."

1. Identify five behaviors you want people to do differently or better. Write them down in the "Undesirable Behaviors" column.
2. Write in the "Desirable Behaviors" column what you want them to do instead. Get clear on the specific alternative behavior.
3. Practice communicating these new phrases so you can be more comfortable speaking them.

Undesirable Behaviors	Desirable Behaviors

Figure 20

CHAPTER 7 ASSESSMENT QUESTIONS:

LACK OF DESIRABLE BEHAVIORS

On a scale of 1-10 (1 = no knowledge or awareness, and 10 = I've been fully aware for a long time), grade yourself on the level of awareness you had on the importance of focusing your communication on "desirable behaviors":

1   2   3   4   5   6   7   8   9   10

On a scale of 1-10 (1 = not very consistent or diligent, and 10 = very consistent and diligent), grade yourself on your consistency and diligence in ensuring all the interpersonal communication interactions you initiate focus on "desirable behaviors":

1   2   3   4   5   6   7   8   9   10

On a scale of 1-10 (1 = not committed at all, and 10 = very committed), grade yourself on your commitment to ensuring all of the interpersonal communication interactions others bring to you only focus on "desirable behaviors" (meaning you expect, encourage, and reinforce communicating with desirable behaviors and hold people accountable to communicating in this manner):

1   2   3   4   5   6   7   8   9   10

What are three areas of your personal and/or professional life where you would gain the biggest benefit using "desirable behaviors"?

1._____

2._____

3._____

RESOURCES

- *Exactly What to Say: The Magic Words for Influence and Impact* by Phil M. Jones

- *Awaken the Giant Within* by Tony Robbins

- *The Influencing Option: The Art of Building a Profit Culture in Business* by Libby Wagner

CHAPTER 8.

LACK OF APPROPRIATE TONE & BODY LANGUAGE

"Brief nasty stares, teasing and jokes that are camouflaged public sham-
ing and insults, who exclude us from minor and major gatherings – all
those nasty little slices of organizational life – don't just hurt for the
moment. They have cumulative effects on our mental health and our
commitment to bosses, peers, and organizations."

–Robert I. Sutton, *The No Asshole Rule*[1]

In Chapter 4: Lack of Immediacy, Urgency, and Promptness, you learned about my egregious communication mistake when I put off having a direct and candid conversation with an employee.

That incident was a factor in my divorce from my first wife, but it was just one of many communication problems I had early in my life and career.

The real communication sin that led to my divorce was my Lack of Appropriate Tone and Body Language. You read about it in the first chapter. When my ex-wife asked me for a divorce, she handed me a book: *The Verbally Abusive Relationship.* The book is

---

1. Robert I. Sutton, *The No Asshole Rule* (New York: Business Plus, 2007), 26-27.

mostly about women who are in verbally abusive relationships with men. I was one of those verbally abusive men.

BUT (and you now know I hate using that word, so when I use it I mean it in the best possible way), there are also often verbally abusive relationships in the workplace. Workplace bullying is a huge problem. I've had to deal with it for a number of small business clients.

Workplace verbal abuse and bullying can stem from different levels, such as your boss, your company owner, or even a colleague.

This bullying can come in many different forms, too, including variations of The 7 Deadliest Communication Sins. For example, Lack of Specificity could be considered bullying if someone purposely withheld information from another as a way to exert control over them.

Lack of Directness and Candor could be considered bullying if someone continually went behind another's back gossiping and complaining about them to others, especially their boss, to undermine their standing or reputation.

Lack of Immediacy, Urgency, and Promptness could be considered bullying if someone continually and purposely waited to the last minute to give another a project, putting extra pressure and stress on them, and making the environment uncomfortable, and maybe even hostile.

Realize though, most times, as with the other communication sins, this verbal abuse is not malicious. It is just a lazy communication habit.

Whether it is malicious or not, this communication sin comes with the risk of instantly destroying the trust in a relationship.

A Brief Look at Workplace Bullying and How it Relates to Some of The 7 Deadliest Communication Sins

Workplace bullying is repeated abuse that creates a psychological power imbalance and an inability for targets to engage in self-defense. It causes psychological and physical harm to targets and witnesses, and monetary losses to the organization.

Bullying is not about having a bad day. Bullying is pervasive and ongoing, and often begins when "the bully" engages in a small slight against someone else, but no one speaks up. Without a reaction, the individual engaging in the bullying has a green light to do it again, and again, and again. Before long, the bully has psychological power over the people he or she is bullying, and these individuals recognize the bully has psychological power over them. It's this psychological power that makes bullying so damaging for people and the organization itself.

Decades of academic research on the topic has shown with overwhelming evidence that people who believe they are being bullied experience anxiety, depression, stress, and other psychological problems, which turn into physical problems too. Of course, as their work suffers, so does the organization—with lowered morale and customer service, decreased production, and increased absenteeism and turnover. In addition, when employers allow legal bad behaviors, such as bullying, to occur, they send the message bad behaviors are tolerated. This increases the organization's chances for lawsuits when illegal behaviors happen, such as harassment.

Bullying behaviors can be categorized into three areas: aggressive communication, humiliation, and manipulation.

Examples of aggressive communication include:

- yelling
- getting into others' personal space
- harsh or aggressive body language or facial expressions
- sending nasty emails

Humiliation includes:

- pointing out mistakes in public
- cc'ing those nasty emails
- consistently asking when a person will quit

Finally, manipulation includes:

- taking a key job task away without explanation
- giving impossible workloads or deadlines
- bottlenecking information
- other passive-aggressive behaviors

People who engage in workplace bullying live in a world of terrible fear that they will be perceived as incompetent, and this is the main drive behind their behavior. Couple that with severely-lacking social and emotional intelligence, and when an employee threatens the bully's competence, the employee is doomed. Thankfully, social and emotional intelligence can be taught, and people who bully can change.

–Catherine Mattice Zundel, MA, SPHR, SHRM-SCP

www.CivilityPartners.com

"THE LOOK"

In my third year as CEO of my first team, we hired a new receptionist for our office. Her name was Allison.

She had only been with us about six weeks when my best friend, Ric, came to the office one afternoon to pick me up to go to lunch. This was the first time Ric had met Allison.

I was on the phone when Ric arrived. While waiting for me to finish, Ric and Allison were getting to know each other.

I hung up the phone, and began walking up the hall. I could hear them talking. As I got to the corner of the hallway to turn into the reception area, though, the two of them went silent.

I asked Allison what she and Ric were talking about.

"Oh, the usual stuff," she said. "We were just getting to know each other."

"That's great," I said, "but I was surprised when got to the corner here, you both stopped talking. I thought that was odd, so I'm wondering what you may have been talking about. Was it me?"

She said, "Well, Ric asked me if, since I've been working here, I've gotten your 'look' yet."

"What are you talking about?" I asked.

"Well," Allison said, "Ric says when you don't like something someone has said or done, you don't say anything to them. You just glare at them."

Immediately, I turned to Ric and just stared at him with a furrowed brow.

Ric began jumping up and down pointing his finger at me, yelling, "That! That's 'the look'! That's what I'm talking about!"

Apparently, I had a "look"–a glare. As Ric later told me, people felt like my eyes were burning a hole right through them.

Until that moment, I had no idea I had a "look."

The feedback was helpful in my development as a leader.

"THE SIGH" AND OTHER FORMS

A look or a glare is just one form of inappropriate tone and body language.

A few years ago, while presenting this topic to the vice presidents of a large New York employer, the VP of Marketing said, "About two weeks ago, three of my direct reports came to my office to confront me about this.

"They said that whenever one or more of them comes to my office to tell me about a problem they need help with, I always sigh. They said that sigh makes them feel like I'm upset with them.

"I told them that wasn't the case at all. I'm not mad at them for bringing me those problems; I'm just diffusing the stress and pressure they've brought to me so I can think more clearly to address it with them.

"I apologized, thanked them for the feedback, and told them I would try to be better in the future."

It was in that session I added "sighing" to my list of inappropriate tone and body language behaviors.

This list includes:

- Eye rolling
- Pointing fingers
- Giving someone the finger
- Folding arms
- Clicking teeth or tongue
- Close talkers
- Raising voices
- Yelling/Shouting
- Sarcasm

Because of these varied behaviors, this is one of The 7 Deadliest Communication Sins that can instantly destroy trust and relationships.

I know. It destroyed my first marriage.

It's destructive in the workplace, too.

One of the primary reasons numerous business owners have hired me is because of inappropriate tone and body language in their work environment.

Workshop participants tell me for some of these–like raised voices, and yelling and shouting–you don't even have to be the direct victim for it to destroy the relationship; you only have to be able to hear it.

An overabundance of such communication can even cause a form of PTSD.

Sometimes, the business owner is the problem. Other times, it's the employees. I've coached for both situations, and helped them to learn a more effective way of communicating.

EMOTIONAL INTELLIGENCE

There are two major causes for the most egregious instances of inappropriate tone and body language.

The first is low self-esteem and insecurity.

People with low self-esteem have a need to protect their ego and to build themselves up. Most times, because their self-esteem is so low, they don't know how. They can't positively build themselves up, so they use inappropriate tone and body language to drag others down.

The second cause is a low level of emotional intelligence.

Emotional intelligence is a concept first coined in the mid-1960s by Michael Beldoch and B. Leuner. It came into prominence through Daniel Goleman's book, *Emotional Intelligence* (1995). Emotional intelligence is "the ability to identify and manage your own emotions and the emotions of others. It is generally said to include three skills: emotional awareness; the ability to harness emotions and apply them to tasks like thinking and problem solving; and the ability to manage emotions, which includes regulating your own emotions and cheering up or calming down other people."[2]

When practicing emotional intelligence, even at a basic level, an individual is able to recognize when a situation is causing an

2. "Emotional Intelligence," *Psychology Today*, last modified 2018, https://www.psychologyto-day.com/us/basics/emotional-intelligence.

emotional response within them, to define that emotion, and to respond more appropriately in the moment.

Typically, people lacking emotional intelligence will react to someone who triggers an internal emotional reaction within them, often through inappropriate tone and body language.

This was my "look."

Interestingly, decades after my "aha" moment with Ric and Allison, I came across another "look" from a client.

My client was the owner of a small company of eight employees, one that serviced fire suppression equipment like fire extinguishers and ventilation units. He too often gave people what they had termed, "the stink eye."

After about three months of working with them and rebuilding trust between my client and his staff, during a team meeting, one of the employees finally confronted his boss about it.

It was presented in a positive, light-hearted manner, and we had a constructive discussion about it. The business owner promised to work on it, and lost "the stink eye."

As I've worked through these situations, and my own challenges as well, I've noticed when we react emotionally in the moment, we are aware of our actions, but we don't realize how our inappropriate tone and body language reactions impact others.

Developing greater emotional intelligence will significantly increase your awareness of your feelings and actions, and so allow you to respond with a more appropriate tone and body language.

THE COST OF TRANSFORMATION

I've been married since 2003 to my second wife, whom I met two years after my divorce. I've shared with her all my flaws and faults from my first marriage. I've told her the horror stories of how I used to verbally berate and yell at my wife during arguments, and put her down with sarcastic, passive-aggressive comments to maintain my control.

"I just can't imagine you being like that," she says.

"Believe it," I say, "because I was, and it cost me about $30,000 to fix, and also my relationship."

It doesn't have to cost that much for you.

That figure is the sum of four years of intensive counseling, coaching, and personal and professional development seminars, as well as all the travel expenses.

It was worth it. I've made great friends along the journey, including finding a new friend in myself.

Before my transformation, I didn't much like myself. I could be triggered into a state of frustration or anger by a single action, comment, or decision from someone else, which was usually my significant other at the time (e.g., my wife). The trigger would send me into a rage of yelling and screaming in close physical proximity to the recipient.

After it was over, I was always remorseful and scared of what I had become in that moment. Fortunately, it never turned physical, but I'm confident my behavior was in no way any less frightening or impactful.

I was so bad, Bruce Springsteen even wrote a song about me. Or, at least as soon as I heard it, I thought it was about me.

It's called *Two Faces.*

The song was on his album, *Tunnel of Love*, released in October, 1987, 14 months before my first wife and I were married, and 10 years before my "second face" caused our divorce.

He writes, "Two faces have I: one that laughs; one that cries. One says hello; one says goodbye. One does things I don't understand. Makes me feel like half a man."[3]

Don't let this communication sin destroy your relationships at work or in your home.

3. Bruce Springsteen, "Two Faces," recorded 1987, Columbia, side 2 track 2 on *Tunnel of Love*, released Oct. 9, 1987, vinyl.

1. Begin developing your Emotional Intelligence by recognizing your triggers and the emotions they generate. Awareness is always the first step to transformation. Use the grid below (See Figure 21)
2. Study, learn and practice how to improve your self-esteem and self-worth. Take a simple, short self-esteem assessment here:
   www.yourchampionshipcompany.com/pages/self-esteem-assessment/

Trigger (Situation/location/person/interaction that brought on the emotion)	Emotion Generated (What emotion(s) did you feel after experiencing this situation?)
(Coworker leaves dirty dishes in office kitchen sink after their lunch)	(Frustration)

Figure 21

ACTION STEPS

1. Ask for Help:

Ask a trustworthy friend or mentor about your tone and body language when you speak with others and how that makes them feel. Remember, I only learned of my "look" and its impact on others because of feedback from someone else.

Also ask what habits or tendencies you have that might negatively impact others. This will build high levels of trust and respect.

For example, say, "I'd like your candid feedback about something–can you tell me if I have any communication habits, in terms of the tone of my voice or body language, that come across as inappropriate and negatively impact my conversations and the impressions people have of me?"

Accept the answers you hear. Simply respond, "Thank you for your help." Then work on improving.

After thirty or sixty days, go back to those people and ask, "How am I doing?" Be sure, when you ask, you are open to hearing their feedback. Ask for specific examples of their experience and what they've noticed in your behavior since the first time you asked. Then, commit to continuing your development in this area.

2. Build Your Emotional Intelligence:

It's important to understand the source of your emotions so you can take control of your reactions.

In my training on Emotional Mastery, I offer a comprehensive program to build these new habits.

The best place to start is to recognize the three main questions your mind asks in every situation that often dictate your reactions:

- What should I focus on?
- What does it mean?
- What should I do?

As you encounter situations, stop yourself and identify the answers to those questions, either in the moment or after in a "self-debriefing." Up to now, you may have been processing them subconsciously in milliseconds.

Now that you are conscious of your mind's process, you will be much more aware of your feelings and habitual reactions. You can start assessing those situations where your tendency is to react with inappropriate tone and body language, and slowly build your emotional intelligence.

CHAPTER 8 ASSESSMENT QUESTIONS

LACK OF APPROPRIATE TONE & BODY LANGUAGE

On a scale of 1-10 (1 = no knowledge or awareness, and 10 = I've been fully aware for a long time), grade yourself on the level of awareness you had on the importance of using appropriate tone and body language when you communicate:

1　2　3　4　5　6　7　8　9　10

On a scale of 1-10 (1 = not very consistent or diligent, and 10 = very consistent and diligent), grade yourself on your consistency and diligence ensuring all the interpersonal communication interactions you initiate are delivered with appropriate tone and body language:

1　2　3　4　5　6　7　8　9　10

On a scale of 1-10 (1 = not committed at all, and 10 = very committed), grade yourself on your commitment to ensuring all of the interpersonal communication interactions others bring to you are delivered with appropriate tone and body language (meaning you expect, encourage, and reinforce communicating with appropriate tone and body language, and hold people accountable to communicating in this manner):

1　2　3　4　5　6　7　8　9　10

What are three areas of your personal and/or professional life where you would gain the biggest benefit when you committed to communicating only with appropriate tone and body language?

1._____

2._____

3._____

RESOURCES

- *Emotional Intelligence* by Daniel Goleman
- *Leadership & Self-Deception* by The Arbinger Institute
- *The No Asshole Rule* by Robert I. Sutton
- *The Asshole Survival Guide* by Robert I. Sutton

CHAPTER 9.

LACK OF FOCUSED ATTENTION

"A person can really only maintain maximum full attention for only four sentences. Whenever you've gone beyond four sentences, be aware that the listener's brain is on over-alert, and he or she is probably getting exhausted... If you want to be heard, keep your statements concise."

—Daniel Goleman, *Emotional Intelligence*[1]

This is the curse of the 21st Century, and it's only going to get worse.

Or, maybe not.

It depends on you.

Have you ever thought about how much attention you feel you need to receive when you communicate with someone?

We expect others to give us their full, focused attention when we are communicating.

How often do we not do the same for others?

1. Daniel Goleman, "How to Overcome Communication Breakdowns," *Emotional Intelligence* (blog), August 23, 2015, http://www.danielgoleman.info/daniel-goleman-how-to-over-come-communication-breakdowns/.

If we are to create an expectation for focused attention, we need to practice what we preach.

Participants in my keynotes and seminars often state other people's "lack of listening" is one of their biggest frustrations.

They are surprised to learn a "lack of listening" is not one of The 7 Deadliest Communication Sins.

Lack of listening is included as a part of this communication sin. It's important to understand listening is not a skill we need to learn.

Listening is a choice, not a skill.

Listening is always a choice. It's a decision we make every minute of every day.

I'm often asked by audience members in my keynotes and workshops, "What about 'active listening skills'?"

I tell them "active listening" isn't really a listening skill; it is a responding skill. You still have to care enough about the person, or what the person is saying, to make the decision to listen.

At a recent half-day workshop for IT professionals at a major U.S. university, one of the participants, Ben, raised his hand. When I called on him, he said, "So what you're saying is, we should actually listen so we can actively listen."

"Yes," I said, "that's exactly right."

You have to actually listen to actively listen.

Distractions prevent us from making that decision to listen. In the 21st Century, there are three primary ways human beings get distracted:

1. Technology
2. Other human beings
3. Our own minds

DISTRACTION 1: TECHNOLOGY

Smartphones, tablets, and other social media communication platforms are the new standard, and even the standard old landline telephone are in global environments and private work cultures, creating an expectation for an instant response.

When we instantly respond, our minds in turn expect an immediate reply. Our dopamine-induced brains seek it; we are distracted until we get it.

We begin wondering, "What happened? Did they not like what I said? What did I say wrong?"

It takes us down a path of negative thoughts, one not productive or positive.

If we happen to be communicating face-to-face with a real human being when that response does comes through, most of us will gravitate towards the incoming notification–be it a ping, a ring, or a tune–and away from the person before us.

Sometimes, it's just a quick glance to see who the notification is from. Sometimes, you get "the hand": hand up, palm out. It means, "Stop what you're saying, because this phone call is more important than you at this moment."

To me, there is nothing more infuriating than being in a conversation with someone when a phone rings or a text tone comes through, and I'm given "the hand."

There is only one cure for this.

When you're in a conversation with another human being in your physical space, put the smart phone away and leave it there.

Allowing yourself to be distracted, be it a phone call or a text, is rude and devalues the person to whom you are speaking.

So many people tell me they hate when this is done to them, and in the same breath, they admit they do it too.

We have to stop!

Remember "the sigh" from Chapter 8? Well, in that same program, Charlotte, the Vice President of Human Resources, told a story related to this communication sin.

In the follow-up debrief after her initial training, Charlotte said, "Since our training on this a couple of weeks ago, I've started holding conversations in my office at my coffee table in the opposite corner from my desk.

"That way, if a call comes in, I can let it go because I can't glance down to see who it is. I know in the past, when I would see it was our CEO calling, I would always pick up the phone."

The CEO, who was also in the session, said, "Don't worry, Charlotte; if I need you, I know where to find you. Focus on the people in front of you."

How many times do we default to dropping what we're doing and jumping in whenever anyone needs us?

Whether it be our boss, a customer, or a co-worker sending us a text or a phone call, we must learn to manage tech interruptions so we can respect and show we value the person in front of us.

DISTRACTION 2: OTHER HUMAN BEINGS

Not all distractions are technical. They may be the other person in front of us, maybe even the physical, human manifestation of the tech interruption.

Do you know a "drive-by" or a "hoverer"? You know, the person who just drops into your doorway while you are on the phone with someone else or are diligently typing away at the keyboard?

They see you're in the middle of something, so they hang there waiting for you to pick your head up.

When you do, instead of excusing themselves and asking if you have a few minutes, they dive in and tell their story, or ask you a detailed question that seems to have no question mark at the end of it.

"The Productivity Pro," Laura Stack, discussed this at a conference I once spoke at. She suggested we "say 'yes' to the person, but 'no' to the interruption."

This means we should respond to our interrupter respectfully by deflecting the present interruption in a way that supports the other person.

You can do this by letting them know, "Now is not a good time. Can we schedule a time later today or tomorrow so I can give you the full attention you deserve?"

Or you could say, "I'm in the middle of something right now. Can I come down to your office in 20 minutes so I can give you the attention you deserve?"

When you do, you will feel you've respected yourself, have greater control over your environment, and will begin to change the expectations of others with regard to how they communicate.

All the while, you will be respecting the other person, too, giving them the attention they deserve, and building trust with them instead of eroding it.

DISTRACTION 3: OUR OWN MIND

Have you ever been in the middle of a conversation with someone standing right in front of you, and you see their mouth moving, but after 15-20 seconds, you realize you have no idea what they said?

This happens all the time in networking situations when we're introduced to new people. They introduce themselves with their name, and maybe their company name or the type of work they do.

You then introduce yourself in a similar fashion.

As the conversation moves forward, you realize you have no idea what this person's name is.

If it's important enough for you to follow up with them, you may ask to exchange business cards, or have them write their name and contact information on the back of your card.

Or, you just let it go for fear of embarrassing yourself or appearing stupid.

This lack of focused attention occurs because you're in your own mind, thinking how you're going to introduce yourself, so you miss their introduction.

Have you ever also noticed, even in regular conversations, you begin engaged, and then after a while realize you've checked out?

Whatever this person was talking about for the last 90 seconds or so, you've missed. They probably either started droning on about things of no value to you, or you began thinking about your own stuff: the project deadline, the kids to pick up from preschool in an hour, the key meeting tomorrow morning you need to prep for, etc.

You've missed what this person in front of you is saying.

Not good.

What can you do to focus your attention in those situations?

THREE TIPS TO ATTAIN GREATER FOCUSED ATTENTION IN YOURSELF & OTHERS

1. Adopt the Belief Multitasking is a Myth

Many people believe they are great at multitasking.

Employers write job descriptions telling people they must be able to multitask.

But, it's really not productive to think in terms of multitasking.

Decades of research continues to show that trying to do multiple things at the same time is not effective, and, in fact, makes us less productive and more stressed.

Research also says while 2% of the population might have a brain hard-wired to truly multitask, most of us do not.

Even those two-percenters who can multitask at real tasks cannot effectively multitask when communicating.

Even if they can, what message is it sending to the person with whom they are communicating?

Remember the last time you were communicating with someone who was multitasking? What did that feel like?

Most people tell me they felt unimportant and devalued.

You cannot multitask when communicating with another human being. Something is going to get the short end of the interaction, and it's typically the person you are hoping to maintain a positive relationship with.

About 10 years ago, I began taking guitar lessons.

Music never interested me until I was in high school, and, even then, it was just your basic "Top 40 Hits" I paid attention to.

Then, I was introduced to Bruce Springsteen and became infatuated with him, his music, and his life. I've been a huge fan for the last 42 years.

After coming home from one of Bruce's 83 live performances I attended in the mid-2000s, I decided I wanted to learn how to do what Bruce did.

I called one of the season ticket holders from my last baseball team, who played in a local rock and roll band. I met with him, bought a guitar, and started learning.

That was true multitasking.

If you play a musical instrument, you know what I'm talking about.

When playing the guitar, you are doing a minimum of two things at the same time. Your right and left hand have to move in coordination with each other. You may also be reading music and lyrics, while tapping your foot for timing.

In this instance, you are doing three or four things simultaneously.

That's real multitasking.

After mastering these things and making some progress, my guitar instructor decided it was time to start singing along with the songs I was playing.

Guess what happened when I started singing as my two arms were playing the guitar?

As soon as I opened my mouth, both my hands stopped moving. It was so frustrating!

I remember playing the introduction to the song, and after playing the four to eight bars of music, I'd open my mouth to sing, and the arms stopped.

Eventually I worked through it, and was able to play and sing (not well for either, though, I have to admit).

That's multitasking.

Everything else is *not* multitasking.

It's "managing multiple priorities."

You are moving from one priority to another. In each moment, you need to give each priority the full attention it requires. Work on it for the necessary time to significantly move it forward, then put it down and move on to the next thing.

2. Learn to "Command" Attention

As a professional speaker, standing on a stage in front of anywhere from five to 1,500 people, it is my responsibility to ensure the audience gives me their focused attention.

I believe it is my responsibility to command their attention, and not their responsibility to give it to me.

It's the same for you.

You must develop the belief the person responsible for ensuring clear communication is the person delivering the communication.

It is not the responsibility of the recipient!

You're probably thinking, "Skip, the other person must be partly responsible, too."

You would be right. But, for the purpose of teaching you to be the most effective communicator you can possibly be, this belief will serve you well.

Commanding the attention of others when you are communicating means:

i. Speak about something of interest to them or something they care about.

To do this, think in terms of "what's in it for them?" when they listen to you speak. Why should they listen to your message?

In sales training, there is an acronym for it, WII-FM, which stands for "What's In It For Me." The acronym represents the call letters for a metaphorical radio frequency all humans tune in to.

Similarly, even before we as humans assess whether we should focus on what others are communicating to us, we will ask another question: "What Does This Mean For Me?" I've termed this metaphorical radio frequency WDTM-FM. It is a question you must answer quickly if you want to maintain your audience's focused attention.

If they don't care, they won't tune in.

Frame your conversation to speak to those two questions, and people will listen to you.

ii. Speak succinctly.

You probably know people who tell long-winded back stories. They give so much information you can't see the relevance or the point they are trying to make.

This is probably when you check out and disengage from the conversation, at least emotionally, and you lose focus while your mind wanders.

A good framework to avoid this is called SBAR (Situation, Background, Assessment, Results). These are the four most important points to communicate your message to your audience.

The first application of SBAR was brought into mainstream business by Doug Bonacum, who in 2008, was the Vice President of Safety Management at Kaiser Permanente.

Bonacum learned the technique in the U.S. Navy, where it was used to facilitate more effective communication between hierarchical levels of authority.

Bonacum recognized challenges in communication between doctors and nurses at Kaiser, and suggested adopting and adapting the SBAR model.

The concept allows for the succinct transfer of information. When speaking, it is recommended to give all four SBAR components in less than 60 seconds.

It takes practice and refinement, and when you adopt it into your speech, and adapt it to your situations, you will command people's attention.

iii. Speak in Bullet Point and Sound Bites

Similar to the SBAR model, practice talking in 15-30 second sound bites of information, allowing opportunities for the other person to engage in the conversation, turning it into a dialogue instead of a monologue.

If you communicate with the intention of the other person being engaged in the conversation, they will be more likely to give you their focused attention and less likely to be distracted.

A related strategy is to chunk your points into three bullet points. It's easy for people to remember a list of three things, rather than a laundry list of unrelated topics.

3. Learn to "Demand" Attention

This does not mean you grab people by the collar, shake them, and yell in their face, "Pay attention to me!"

This does mean you ask for their attention.

Simply say, "John, this is really important, and I need your focused attention on this so we can make a decision before the end of today. Is now a good time for us to discuss it, or do you need us to find a better time later today?"

This sets the expectation that what you are going to speak with John about is important, and requires him to pay attention for a particular reason.

It is showing you respect their situation and are not expecting them to drop everything in the moment for you.

You can also do this in meetings.

So many meetings are ineffective because there is no expectation for participation.

I could write an entire book on how to run more effective meetings, but for now, simply realize you can set an intention at the beginning of every meeting regarding the focused attention of attendees, such as:

"The purpose of this meeting is X. So that we can achieve X within the next 45 minutes and you can get back to your other priorities, it is going to require everyone's focused attention. By that, I mean turn your smartphones and tablets off so we can all focus on the issue at hand. I promise you will get a tech-check break in 45 minutes."

The 60-Second SBAR Status Update

Example:
Construction update on a baseball stadium project in relation to Opening Day

Situation:
Opening Day is June 18, giving us less than four months to build our stadium. We're still waiting for the county legislature to approve the funding. We've sold out all advertising and sponsorships, and we've capped season ticket sales so we have enough for individual game purchasers.

Background:

The construction manager needs 90 days to build something that will host 4,500 people. At best, we'll have temporary concessions stands that can sell pre-packaged food. But the good news is the restrooms will be his priority to comply with the county public health department.

Assessment:

We need a contingency plan in case we can't get it done for June 18th, one that includes an alternative playing site and financial resources for cash flow if we have to give back deposits or hold it in escrow for next season.

Recommendation:

I recommend we alert the league president, discuss options for playing home games on the road for some or all of this season, and begin negotiating some type of revenue split with the teams that will be hosting our "home" games.

CAVEAT

You must fulfill your end of the promise and end the meeting at the 45-minute mark (or whatever determined time) to build trust for next time.

Human beings are highly suggestible. This means if you craft your language in the right way, you can influence people to do things they wouldn't do otherwise.

It's as simple as asking someone to do a favor for you. You've probably done this often in your life. The person you are asking isn't necessarily thinking about doing anything on your behalf, or even thinking there is a need to do anything on your behalf.

Then a need arises and you go up to someone minding their own business to say, "I have to go to a meeting right now, and don't have time to put this package together and take it to the post office. It needs to go out in today's mail and I'm going to be tied up in my meeting till after 5:00 p.m. today. Could you do me a favor and make sure this gets out in today's mail?"

Chances are, if you have a decent relationship with the person, and even if you don't but work for the same company, they will accept your request and fulfill it for you.

Suggest people do things that are in their best interests, and you can respectfully *demand* and receive their focused attention.

SOLUTIONS TO PRACTICE

Choose to listen, and commit to eliminating distractions for yourself in each of these three areas:

1. Technology: Turn off your cell phone or simply don't bring it with you to meetings or when you know you will be having a conversation. Fully engage with the person or people in front of you.
2. Other People: Practice respectfully talking with the people who may be distracting you. For example, say, "Now is not a good time. Can we schedule a time later today or tomorrow so I can give you the full attention you deserve?"
3. Your Own Mind: Identify times when you multitask. What can you do to change that habit? Prioritize your tasks, and choose to focus on one thing at a time for a set amount of time.

ACTION STEPS

1. Start with the simple practice of "demanding" or asking others' attention:

   - Tune into the WII-FM and WDTM-FM frequencies of your audience.
   - Write down why they should listen ("what's in it for them").
   - During your speech, focus your language around the interests of your audience.

2. Practice "commanding" communication techniques to build the habit.

   - Speak in 30-second sound bites.

- Speak and write using succinct bullet points (no more than three).
- Apply SBAR technique to situational updates and handoffs.

CHAPTER 9 ASSESSMENT QUESTIONS

LACK OF APPROPRIATE FOCUSED ATTENTION

On a scale of 1-10 (1 = no knowledge or awareness, and 10 = I've been fully aware for a long time), grade yourself on the level of awareness you had on the importance of applying focused attention in your interpersonal communication interactions:

1 2 3 4 5 6 7 8 9 10

On a scale of 1-10 (1 = not very consistent or diligent, and 10 = very consistent and diligent), grade yourself on your consistency and diligence ensuring all the interpersonal communication interactions you initiate are providing focused attention:

1 2 3 4 5 6 7 8 9 10

On a scale of 1-10 (1 = not committed at all, and 10 = very committed), grade yourself on your commitment to ensuring all of the interpersonal communication interactions others bring to you are engaged with focused attention (meaning you expect, encourage, and reinforce communicating with focused attention, and hold people accountable to communicating in this manner):

1 2 3 4 5 6 7 8 9 10

What are three areas of your personal and/or professional life where you would gain the biggest benefit when you commit to providing focused attention in your interpersonal communication interactions?

1._____

2._____

3._____

RESOURCES

- *What to Do When There is Too Much to Do* by Laura Stack
  www.TheProductivityPro.com/WhatToDo

- *Focus: The Hidden Driver of Excellence* by Daniel Goleman

- *How to Win Friends & Influence People* by Dale Carnegie

PART IV.

YOUR NEXT LEVEL - USING COMMUNICATION TO BUILD CHAMPIONSHIP COMPANY PERFORMANCE

"Effective teamwork begins and ends with communication. Communication does not always occur naturally, and must be taught and practiced in order to bring everyone together as one. The most crucial element of communicating is telling the truth."

–Coach K (Mike Krzyzewski)
Duke University, Head Basketball Coach[1]

---

1. Power Forward, "Coach K: The Importance of Communication," *Forward Thinking* (blog), March 30, 2017, https://gopowerforward.com/blog/coach-k-importance-of-communication/.

CHAPTER 10.

MASTERING THE 3 LEVELS OF COMMUNICATION INFLUENCE

"Communication is a skill that you can learn. It's like riding a bicycle or typing. If you're willing to work at it, you can rapidly improve the quality of every part of your life."

–Brian Tracy

Now that you have an awareness of The 7 Deadliest Communication Sins and how they are causing most or all of your miscommunications, misunderstandings, and frustrations with others, you're ready to expand your ability to communicate to influence.

Interpersonal communication occurs at three primary levels, called The Communication Influence Pyramid (See Figure 22).

The best leaders become the best leaders by mastering The Communication Influence Pyramid. They communicate effectively, and are comfortable communicating across all three levels.

When you understand the three levels in the pyramid below, and begin applying your new insights about The 7 Deadliest Communication Sins to each of the levels, you can transform your ability to communicate in 21 different contexts.

Imagine how powerful a communicator you will be when you are able master both The 7 Deadliest Communication Sins and The Communication Influence Pyramid!

Figure 22

LEVEL 1: THE FOUNDATION

SELF-COMMUNICATION

The pyramid is first built on the Foundation level, which is our own self-communication.

There is only one person with whom you communicate 24 hours a day, seven days a week, 52 weeks a year, every year of your life.

You.

Do you often find yourself using language like, "I can't…," "I don't like…," or, "I'm worried about…"? Do you often find yourself doubting your abilities? These are are all signs of negative self-communication, and can become self-fulfilling prophecies.

In order to lay a strong communication foundation, you need to change your self-talk. How? Begin to look for solutions instead of problems. Look at the likely potential for positive outcomes instead of focusing on the downsides and risks.

Your self-communication drives everything. Mastering it is the key to your happiness and success in every area of your life.

Even the great masters of self-communication will tell you it is a never-ending journey of focused work. If you're struggling with it, that's okay. Be kind to yourself on your journey.

Take your time to learn and build this communication skill. As the base of the pyramid, self-communication impacts every area of your life, as well as your ability to influence others in the next two levels. It is important to develop a solid foundation.

LEVEL 2: THE TRUST BUILDER

1:1, PDR COMMUNICATION

This level is called The Trust Builder, because trust is what is required to be able to exert a positive influence on people in your sphere of influence, personally and professionally.

When you master this level, you will be able to connect with others in one-on-one settings. You will also come across as authentic and genuine, and be able to present yourself in a way that puts others at ease. Not only will others like you, but you will build trust with them quickly, and for all the right reasons.

PDR Communication represents an important model within this level, and refers to a "Prompt, Direct, & Respectful" approach to communicating in a one-on-one relationship (See *Chapter 5: A Lack of Directness and Candor*).

Learning about the The 7 Deadliest Communication Sins has already equipped you with strategies and tools to grow in your PDR Communication.

As you begin to implement those strategies, you will notice other people begin to respond to you differently.

You are going to exert a more positive influence, just by applying the communication strategies you've learned in this book.

You have much more to learn in this area. There are more communication tips, tools, and techniques (listed in the Resources section of each chapter) in this level that will allow you to accelerate your ability to build trust quickly with others and frame your language even more specifically to exert positive influence.

LEVEL 3: THE IMPRESSION MAKER

PUBLIC COMMUNICATION

At some point during our career, we all have to engage in the Impression Maker level. One way or another, you will make a public impression. It behooves you to grow in competence and confidence in public communication to begin making favorable impressions.

There are three contexts where people can exert positive influence while communicating in public:

1. Public speaking: presenting and giving speeches in front of the room

2. Facilitating/leading meetings
3. Group sharing: speaking around the conference room table or in another group setting

Each context has its own unique strategies, skills, and techniques for maximum impact and impression.

Many people tell me they have a fear of public speaking and avoid it like the plague, yet often must because their boss expects it.

In those situations, people either do not prepare and wing it, or prepare but apply bad techniques. Both approaches result in leaving a negative impression.

Leading and facilitating meetings may be even more important than presenting in front of the room, simply because you will probably have many more opportunities to lead and run meetings than give presentations.

Wouldn't you like to have the reputation for running effective meetings? If you do, it will make a huge impression on others. Imagine if people gave you feedback that they enjoyed attending your meetings!

Finally, it is vital to learn how to effectively communicate in a group-sharing situation.

This setting may be the best opportunity to speak your mind, and it's important to learn how to have your voice heard even when you aren't in front.

Mastering The 3 Levels of Communication Influence is the next level of your communication growth and development.

You can start this stage of your development by going to www.CommunicationPowerForLeaders.com to learn more about the digital training program.

Readers of this book can get it at a 67% discount. The regular price is $297.

At the site, you can also access the entire 10 hours of audio training recordings and the workbooks for each level for just $97.

Use coupon code **7sinsbook** when you check out.

CHAPTER 11.

THE END GAME

"Champions are not the ones who always win races – champions are the ones who get out there and try. And try harder the next time. And even harder the next time. 'Champion' is a state of mind. They are devoted. They compete to best themselves as much if not more than they compete to best others. Champions are not just athletes."

–Simon Sinek

Back in Chapter 2, I spoke strongly about setting a new standard for your communication. This closing chapter is about what can happen when you do.

I'm hopeful that by now you've seen how The 7 Deadliest Communication Sins impact your relationships, both in and out of the workplace.

Whether you are in a small business work environment, on a small team in a large work environment, or in a family, you can probably understand how the cumulative effects of these common communication mistakes can cause damage, both short- and long-term.

As you also read early on, the goal should be to shoot for constant and never-ending improvement in your communication habits across these seven categories, and not to expect you will eliminate them from the face of the earth. Figure 23 shows the three mindsets that define every single one of our communications; it is our responsibility to be aware of them, to manage them, and to work through them, for the benefit of our teams, our friends, our family, and ourselves.

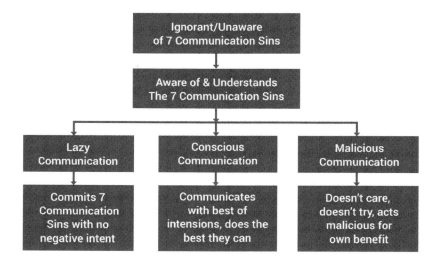

Figure 23

You can, at best, hope to reduce their frequency and impact by committing to raising your standard for what you expect from your own communication and those around you.

The best thing to do now is commit to that new standard, and build new habits of communication.

The best approach is to pick one of the seven sins to focus on for the next 70 days.

Why 70 days?

Two reasons. First, someone once proclaimed if you repeated a behavior for 21 days, you can build that behavior into new habit. Quite frankly, based on personal experience, I don't think that's enough time.

Secondly, Alan Weiss, a coach, mentor, and trainer to solo practitioner consultants, many years ago taught me The 1% Solution. He explains simply on his blog, "I believe in The 1% Solution: Improve by 1% a day, and in 70 days you're twice as good."[1] If you improve one percent per day in one particular area, based on the power of compound interest, in 70 days, Weiss claims you will be twice as good. I try to practice it regularly.

After 70 days, you can move on to your second communication sin, and so on.

In 16 months, or 1.3 years, you will double your communication effectiveness, all the while building (or rebuilding) relationships based on high credibility and high trust.

YOU CAN'T DO IT ALONE

As you begin building new habits across these seven communication categories, you are going to notice everyone around you committing these communication sins. It's going to become hard for you to tolerate your environment.

A time will come when you will feel the pull to exert positive influence on those in your environment.

When I wrote my white paper report in 2011, and started speaking to small business leaders on these strategies to help them

1. Alan Weiss, "About This Blog," *Alan's Blog: Architect of Professional Communities* (blog), last modified 2018, http://www.contrarianconsulting.com/about-this-blog/.

communicate to motivate, I encouraged them to take what they learned and share it with their staff.

Imagine if you took this book and had a weekly meeting to review and discuss The 7 Deadliest Communication Sins? Imagine if you had your entire team apply The 1% Solution to each communication sin?

Communicating with these strategies, tips, tools, and techniques will make any of the communication sins irrelevant. When high levels of trust have been developed among coworkers, between employees and superiors, and company leadership, any time someone commits a communication sin, everyone has the tools to immediately address it, and work through it in a way that continues to build and reinforce trust.

That's the essence and the foundation of a company culture that can deliver high-performance, championship-level results.

THE POTENTIAL

In Chapter 2, I made the claim, "communication is the cause of every success, failure, and frustration you experience. Therefore, it's time to raise your standard for what you expect from communication from yourself and those around you."

Remember the stories from Chapters 3 and 4 about the service technicians in the field who received mixed messages and delayed decisions from the company owner?

Jerry, the owner of this small business, came to me while I was delivering a seminar on creating a Championship Company Culture.

We had a spirited discussion about performance management and employee motivation strategies. He was lamenting the fact he couldn't motivate his field technicians to participate in helping market the company while they were on construction sites.

He told me, and the rest of the seminar attendees, about how he had tried "everything" (see "Beware of Universals, Absolutes, and Exaggerations" in Ch. 3). Jerry let us all know how frustrated he was with the motivation, or lack thereof, from his technicians resisting his job requirements to help sell projects for the company.

When Jerry and I spoke again after the seminar, our discussion changed significantly. He was much more forthcoming with issues and frustrations.

He told me had just fired one of his technicians, who had been with him for about six years, and was ready to fire another who was his longest-serving employee of 14 years.

After our successful project, Stan, this veteran employee, went from on the verge of being fired and looking for other job opportunities (since he also wasn't happy with the situation) to becoming the most productive employee in bringing in direct referrals from the field.

When I met Jerry and his team, the company had dropped from about $800,000 in annual revenue to about $650,000. When we finished our work together, the company had its best revenue year ever at $880,000–an increase of 35% in just 18 months.

While recapping our work, Jerry reminded me of the day we had met at my seminar. He said, "When I first came to you with the problems I was facing, you immediately told me, 'Jerry, that sounds like a communication problem.' And, that's exactly what it turned out to be."

Jerry, according to his employees, was sending mixed messages and causing confusion around what was most important. When this happens, employees can't possibly perform at their best, and they develop low morale, which leads to low motivation on the job.

This, as you read in Chapter 3, this comes from Communication Sin #1: Lack of Specificity.

Jerry also suffered from Communication Sin #2: Lack of Urgency, Immediacy, and Promptness. This sin affected his ability to make decisions on issues brought to him by employees and on basic company strategy.

As the trust in relationships between Jerry and his key employees slowly eroded, other communication sins crept in.

Over 18 months, the team gradually practiced the communication strategies you've read about in this book. With that gradual improvement, over time, Jerry and his staff built new habits of communication, which resulted in significant financial results.

I worked with Jerry and his team to set a new standard for how they communicated with, and what they expected from, each other. Our relationship included monthly training, coaching, and consistent support.

This pattern is typical.

For Jay and Betty, in a small manufacturing firm, this pattern also emerged.

In that environment, there had been a long history of discord between Betty and two other key team members–discord had created historic levels of toxicity. It was the worst I had seen in 15 years of this work.

Jay inherited all those employees and relationships when he took over the company, seven years before I met him. Jay did the best he could with the resources he had, and got the environment to an artificially-improved state.

It was artificial in the sense he was able to quell the intensity and the emotional outbursts to a degree, but there would still be weekly explosions of negative emotion between employees in the open work environment.

The underlying core issues were not being addressed; they were being suppressed.

That's what most of us do: we suppress instead of address.

That, ladies and gentleman, is Communication Sin #3: A Lack of Directness and Candor.

In Jay and Betty's situation, I facilitated numerous weekly meetings with the five members of the company's leadership team, teaching them communication concepts, skills, and helping them set up agreements as to how they would address issues between them.It wasn't easy, and there were times when, in the moment, I honestly didn't know what I was doing or what would work. Fortunately, I had enough tools in my tool belt to keep bringing things to bear on a situation until something worked. One of my most powerful tools, it turned out, didn't seem to be a tool at all.

It was silence.

Frankie Valli and The Four Seasons had a hit song in the 1960s called *Silence is Golden*. I didn't realize how true it was until that moment.

We were at a crossroads in building a bridge between Betty and another leadership team member, Tsuniu. Their relationship was rife with conflict. He, Betty, and I were in the conference room alone, discussing ways they could better serve each other.

I posed a question to try to understand why Tsuniu struggled with communicating and working with her. We sat in silence as Tsuniu pondered the question. I could tell he was in a state of not wanting to speak for fear it would make things worse.

We've all been there, thinking, "If I say something, it's going to make things worse. It's going to blow up because I know how that other person feels and thinks. Do I want to go there? What good will it do?"

Waiting in silence, with Betty chomping at the bit to say something or ask something more of Tsuniu, I used non-verbal communication, eye contact, and a hand gesture to keep Betty at bay, remaining in silence.

It seemed like hours, but it was probably less than two minutes.

Finally, Tsuniu said, "I feel like Betty is always trying to get me in trouble."

This was a breakthrough.

This had been Tsuniu's belief about Betty for more than 10 years.

No wonder they couldn't get along.

Tsuniu's comments opened the floodgates of direct and candid communication that has transformed their relationship and their work environment.

Suppressing feelings and beliefs means you are not addressing them. When suppressed, they are lying dormant under the surface, and will not only rise to the surface when under pressure, but explode.

This was the toxic work environment in which Jay, Betty, and Tsuniu had lived every workday for more than 10 years.

These case studies are just a few of the projects I've worked on, with similar beginnings and similar successful endings.

Sadly, they are just a few of the millions of toxic work environments that are still widespread in the workplaces of every industry today.

The cause is communication.

Not "lack of communication"– remember, there is no such thing as a "lack of communication." We are always communicating.

The cause is *how* we are communicating. All problems can be directly linked back to one or more of The 7 Deadliest Communication Sins, and all successes can always be related to the solutions, when people choose to apply more positive, productive, and effective communication skills.

Now you know what the challenges are, and what solutions to apply.

When you do, you will be on your way to building a more positive, more productive, and even more profitable company or team, one that performs with consistent excellence, and delivers championship level results.

FINAL THOUGHTS

Congratulations! You've made it to the end!

You are truly committed to improving your communication as an organization leader, be it of a small business, a large corporation, non-profit, or your own life and family.

Remember these seven deadliest communication mistakes will never go away. You will never eliminate them from your interpersonal communication. They are human nature.

The power of this book and my keynotes and seminars is that it raises your awareness of them.

The next step is to decrease how frequently you commit each of the seven communication sins, and so reduce the impact they have on yourself and others.

You have that power now.

Use this book as a guide to building your Communication Power.

Pick one of the seven communication sins to work on each month. Tell your team members and your family members what you're doing, and ask them to hold you accountable.

Better yet, engage your team in a conversation about improving communication among everyone. Use these seven communication sins as a framework for that conversation, and ask the team which of the seven they'd like to begin with.

Here's a tip: Start at the beginning, because working on reducing the lack of specificity between your team members will give you the biggest bang for your efforts.

Imagine if everyone on your team was focused on, committed, and held accountable to communicating with greater specificity.

My work with clients just like you, helping teams to do just that, increases productivity by 50%.

If you'd like help integrating the awareness of The 7 Deadliest Communication Sins into your work environment, I'd welcome the opportunity to explore with you the ways we can make that happen, including:

- Webinars
- Facilitated strategic work sessions via video conferencing

- Lunch & Learns (live or video conference)
- Seminars and live strategic work sessions on-site
- Keynote speeches for your next corporate event
- Individual executive communication or team coaching.

I wish you well on your transformative journey. If you'd like additional help, visit us at www.YourChampionshipCompany.com or give us a call at 845-463-3838 to explore how to bring Communication Power to your company or organization.

ABOUT THE AUTHOR

SKIP WEISMAN

Skip's first career was in the industry of his childhood dream: professional baseball. His disappointment at being cut from his 9th grade baseball team tryouts fueled his desire to find any other way to stay close to the game he loved.

Earning a master's degree in sports administration and facility management (Ohio University, 1982) was his ticket to a 20-year career in baseball. After an internship and three years apprenticing as an assistant general manager, Skip, at 26 years old, found himself in the right place at the right time and was promoted to vice president, general manager, and CEO of his first baseball team in Greensboro, North Carolina.

After the 1993 season, Skip fulfilled the dream of every baseball operator: to build a professional baseball franchise from the ground up in a new market with a new stadium. While serving as president of the Erie Sailors team in Erie, Pennsylvania, the franchise was recruited by Dutchess County, New York, and the team became the Hudson Valley Renegades.

Twice in his baseball leadership career, he was recognized by national industry publications. The first was in 1987 when *The Sporting News* selected Skip as its Executive of the Year for all of

Class A Minor League baseball. Then, in 1998, his Hudson Valley Renegades were recognized by *Baseball America* as its Short-Season Class A Organization of the Year.

For personal lifestyle reasons, Skip decided to leave his baseball career behind after the 2001 season to open his company Weisman Success Resources, Inc.

Since 2006, Skip has focused his company's efforts towards working with small business owners and their teams to improve communication in the workplace. This improved communication in turn leads to a more positive work environment, creating higher productivity, and ultimately producing greater revenue and profits.

In 2017, Skip formalized his methodology under the banner of The Small Business Championship Game Plan, which provides a systematic process to create championship performance in small businesses.

Skip is an internationally recognized professional speaker on the topic of leadership and workplace communication and creating championship teams in small businesses. His signature keynote topics include:

- A New Standard for Workplace Communication: Overcoming the 7 Deadliest Communication SINs
- Mastering the 3 Levels of Communication Influence: How the Best Leaders Become the Best Leaders
- The 5 Steps to Creating Championship Performance in a Small Business Work Environment

ACKNOWLEDGMENTS

This is not the book I intended to write, and I am so appreciative to Kent Gustavson of Blooming Twig for seeing the value in this topic. In 2011, I wrote a white paper report on The 7 Deadliest Communication Sins that launched my professional speaking business. The topic has been my signature keynote speech and seminar ever since. I thought it was time to move on to a new topic and leave this one behind. But Kent encouraged me to go with this one first.

He said it would be easy. He lied. But I am so thankful he did. Writing this book with his guidance and encouragement has allowed me to dig deeper than I thought possible into this topic, and all of my future teachings will be even better for my audiences because of it.

This book would not have been possible without all the clients I've had the privilege to serve and to learn from. Many people say they learn as much or more from their coaching and consulting clients than their clients do from them. That is so true in my case. I got into this field by accident, thanks to a referral to a small business owner who needed some help fixing a toxic work environment. He took a chance on me and changed my business and life forever. Every client since has continued to build my understanding of human motivation in the workplace, and pushes me to find ways to break through situations that at the outset seem unfixable.

Thanks to all my friends and colleagues, some who know me personally, and some who don't: your books have inspired me. Thank you for allowing me to borrow quotes and share your voices to reinforce my own message here in this book.

Thanks to Joe Beccalori, Corinne Courtney, Cameron Farruggia, Dawn Kirspel, Michael Petrone, Daniel Pink, and Jim Williamson for taking the time to read and review the manuscript, and for all of your suggestions and encouraging feedback.

Specific thanks to Catherine Mattice Zundel, who went above and beyond writing that vignette on workplace bullying, a topic that has received too little attention over the years. I hope Catherine's contribution here will help raise more awareness on this issue, and help Catherine gain a wider audience for the important work she is doing.

Thanks to the editing team at Blooming Twig, Emily and Gabriella, who pushed me for more details and better refinement to help make my content even richer.

And, last but certainly not least, big thanks to my wife, Anne Saylor, who has made my life joyous and fun since our first date on January 11, 2000, for supporting me in my business endeavors, and for tolerating the ups and downs of it all over the years.